Robots

OTHER TITLES IN THE TECHNOLOGY 360 SERIES:

Cell Phones
Online Social Networking
Video Games

Robots

Jenny MacKay

LUCENT BOOKS
A part of Gale, Cengage Learning

GALE
CENGAGE Learning™

Detroit • New York • San Francisco • New Haven, Conn • Waterville, Maine • London

LIBRARY OF CONGRESS CATALOGING-IN-PUBLICATION DATA

MacKay, Jenny, 1978-
    Robots / by Jenny MacKay.
        p. cm. -- (Technology 360)
    Includes bibliographical references and index.
    ISBN 978-1-4205-0168-1 (hardcover)
    1. Robots--Juvenile literature. I. Title.
    TJ211.2.M325 2010
    629.8'92--dc22

                  2009045634

Lucent Books
27500 Drake Rd
Farmington Hills MI 48331

ISBN-13: 978-1-4205-0168-1
ISBN-10: 1-4205-0168-2

Printed in the United States of America
1 2 3 4 5 6 7 14 13 12 11 10

Printed by Bang Printing, Brainerd, MN, 1st Ptg., 05/2010

CONTENTS

FOREWORD

"As we go forward, I hope we're going to continue to use technology to make really big differences in how people live and work."
—Sergey Brin, cofounder of Google

The past few decades have seen some amazing advances in technology. Many of these changes have had a direct and measurable impact on the way people live, work, and play. Communication tools, such as cell phones, satellites, and the Internet, allow people to keep in constant contact across longer distances and from the most remote places. In fields related to medicine, existing technologies—digital imaging devices, robotics, and lasers, for example—are being used to redefine surgical procedures and diagnostic techniques. As technology becomes more complex, however, so have the related ethical, legal, and safety issues.

Psychologist B.F. Skinner once noted that "the real problem is not whether machines think but whether men do." Recent advances in technology have, in many cases, drastically changed the way people view the world around them. They can have a conversation with someone across the globe at lightning speed, access a huge amount of information with the click of a key, or become an avatar in a virtual world of their own making. While advances like these have been viewed as a great boon in some quarters, they have also opened the door to questions about whether or not the speed of technological advancement has come at an unspoken price. A closer examination of the evolution and use of these devices provides a deeper understanding of the social, cultural, and ethical implications that they may hold for our future.

The Lucent Books' Technology 360 series not only explores how evolving technologies work, but also examines the short- and long-term impact of their use on society as a whole. Each volume in Technology 360 focuses on a particular invention, device, or family of similar devices, exploring how the device was developed, how it works, its impact on society, and its possible future uses. Volumes also contain a timeline specific to each topic, a glossary of terms used in the text, and a subject index. Sidebars, photos, and detailed illustrations, tables, charts and graphs help further illuminate the text.

Titles in this series feature inventions and devices familiar to most readers, such as robots, digital cameras, iPods, and video games. Not only will users get an easy-to-understand, "nuts and bolts" overview of these inventions, they will also learn just how much these devices have evolved. For example, in 1973 a Motorola cell phone weighed about 2 pounds (0.9kg) and cost four thousand dollars. Today cell phones weigh only a few ounces and are often inexpensive enough for every member of the family to have one. Lasers—long a staple of the industrial world—have become highly effective surgical tools, capable of reshaping the cornea of the eye and cleaning clogged arteries. Early video games were played on large machines in arcades; today games are played on sophisticated home systems that allow for multiple players and cross-location networking.

IMPORTANT DATES

330 B.C. Greek author Aristotle describes cogwheels, an ancestor of modern robot gears, in his book *Mechanical Problems*.

270 B.C. Greek engineer Ctesibius uses pneumatics and hydraulics to make a musical organ and a mechanical water clock.

1495 Renaissance artist Leonardo da Vinci draws detailed blueprints for a mechanical knight.

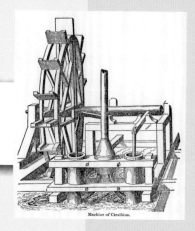

Machine of Ctesibius.

1941– 1942 Science fiction writer Isaac Asimov predicts the rise of a powerful robot industry and describes three laws of robotics, the first code of ethics for robots, in a short story titled "Runaround."

1961 The first industrial robot, Engelberger and Devol's Unimate, goes to work on the assembly line of a General Motors car factory in Trenton, New Jersey.

1945 **1955** **1965**

1921 Karel Čapek's play *R.U.R. (Rossum's Universal Robots)* opens in Czechoslovakia, popularizing the word "robot" to describe a mechanical man.

1956 Engineer Joseph Engelberger and inventor George Devol create the world's first robot company, Unimation, Inc.

1970 Shakey, the first mobile robot controlled by artificial intelligence, is produced by the Stanford Research Institute in California.

1951 Inventor W. Grey Walter reveals his robotic "tortoises" at the Festival of Britain.

1977 HILARE robot is invented in Toulouse, France, and the Stanford CART robot is invented at Stanford University in California. Both use cameras to navigate in cluttered spaces without human help.

in the Development of Robots

1988 Scientists at the Massachusetts Institute of Technology (MIT) build Genghis, a six-legged walking robot.

2002 iRobot introduces the vacuuming robot Roomba.

2008 MIT invents Nexi, a robot that shows feelings and interprets the emotions of people around it.

1994 Dante II, a walking robot built at Carnegie Mellon University's Robotics Institute, explores an active volcano in Alaska.

1999 Probotics Inc. invents a personal robot called Cye that can be programmed to do household chores and recharges its own batteries as needed.

2009 A British submarine robot called Nereus explores the Challenger Deep, the deepest known ocean trench in the world.

1985   **1995**   **2005**

1997 NASA's space exploration robot Sojourner arrives on Mars in the *Pathfinder* space shuttle and begins exploring the planet's surface.

2000 The da Vinci Surgical System, made by Intuitive Surgical, Inc., becomes the first robotic surgical system approved by the U.S. Food and Drug Administration (FDA) to perform surgery.

2009 Artificial intelligence engineers at Robert Gordon University in the United Kingdom build a robotic brain that grows as it learns, thus evolving over time.

2006 NASA builds a teleoperated space astronaut named Robonaut.

Manufactured Servants

Manmade machines make life easier for people. They operate in almost every room of people's homes and businesses. They provide transportation by land, sea, and air. In most countries of the world, essential items, such as food and clothing, are harvested or made by machines. As technology improves, new machines are invented that can do much more complicated and difficult things, and human interest in and dependence on them increases.

Some of the earliest recorded human history describes people inventing and using new machines and imagining manmade servants, independent machines that could do useful, difficult, or boring work for people. Through the years, many people have dreamed of such machines living side by side with the human population as helpful companions. Other people have worried that intelligent machines, built to be truly independent, could rise up against their human creators. Both versions of the machine-servant, the helpful and the frightening, have appeared in literature since the time of the ancient Egyptians, Greeks, and Romans, but it was not until the twentieth century that inventors finally created the first automatic, "thinking" machines. These were called robots, stemming from the word *robota*, which roughly means slave labor.

The development of modern robots began in the mid-1900s, when scientists built the first metal bodies with

moving parts. The first truly useful robots were basically just mechanical arms bolted to tables or floors and programmed to do repetitive tasks. These stationary robots were built to replace human workers in difficult, boring, or dangerous factory jobs. Roboticists, scientists who design and build robots, then began experimenting with mechanical bodies that moved around on wheels, used video cameras to see, were powered by batteries, and had computerized brains to think. The first independently mobile robots were slow and klutzy and had very limited intelligence. However, they were a successful step in a new scientific field called robotics: the design, construction, operation, and application of machines that behave like living things.

Advanced robots that can do more than just roll back and forth on their wheels have evolved side by side with advances in technology and computer science that give robots more

Automobile companies were one of the first industries to incorporate robots into their assembly line work flow.

physical abilities and help them process complicated information. Technological developments that brought about smaller, faster computers with many times the processing power of early models also allowed roboticists to create faster machines with powerful computerized brains. Just as they have artificial bodies, these robots also have artificial intelligence. Their mechanical parts and joints are often designed like those of living creatures, flexing and bending the way animals' limbs do, and robots can even be programmed to do helpful things.

Modern robots accomplish tasks that are difficult or impossible for people to do, from exploring volcanoes to working in outer space. As computers grow ever more powerful, robots, too, become smarter. Although they do not fully think and feel for themselves, some scientists predict that in the twenty-second century, such advancement is possible. Eventually, there may be robots that are just as smart as people. The human dream of manmade companions, thousands of years in the making, is becoming a reality. Some people fear the consequences of building a machine that thinks on its own. Other people believe robots have the potential to vastly improve the human experience. One thing almost everyone can agree on, however, is that robots are fascinating.

CHAPTER 1

The History of Robots

T he first robots, manmade machines that move independently and respond to their surroundings, were not invented until the twentieth century, but the concept has existed for thousands of years, dating back at least to ancient Egypt. When wealthy and important Egyptians died, they were buried with *shabti*, mummylike miniature statues that people believed would act as servants in the afterlife. The wealthier an Egyptian was at the time of death, the more *shabti* were placed in his tomb. The *shabti*, it was thought, would do all the work in the afterlife so the deceased could relax and enjoy eternity. "Egyptians believed the shabti would perform what we would describe today as robotic action: automatically rising when called to work, and returning to rest afterward,"[1] says science and technology historian Lisa Nocks.

The idea of human models to do people's bidding gained momentum among the ancient Greeks, whose storytelling traditions around the year 1000 B.C. included tales of intelligent machines that acted as servants to the gods. In his epic story *The Iliad*, Greek author Homer wrote about female servants made of gold who were intelligent and could converse. His story also featured wheel-driven, three-legged stools that moved automatically to serve meals to the gods. No such device yet existed, but these stories of robotic servants inspired the Greeks to develop some of the first automated machines, using simple technology and concepts of physics that are still integral to the robots of today.

Early Machines

A machine is any device that transmits force, movement, or energy, making it easier for a person to accomplish a difficult task. "A machine does not do away with the need to exert

Early machines, like the cogwheel, were developed to make a difficult task easier to accomplish. Pictured here is a modern-day use of the cogwheel: bicycle gears.

THE COGWHEEL

Some robots still use the ancient concept of cogwheels to form gears that turn wheels and other moving parts. A cogwheel is a special wheel that has teeth, or pegs, around its circumference. When one cogwheel is set in motion against another, the teeth act as levers against the teeth of the second wheel and force both wheels to turn in opposite directions. The sizes of the two wheels may vary to make the gear turn faster or slower.

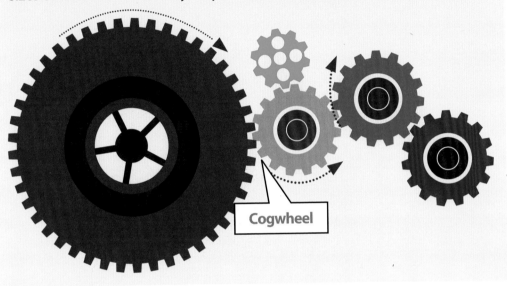

Cogwheel

effort," says Nocks, "but by helping to distribute weight or create leverage, it makes the effort more productive than the exclusive use of muscle power."[2] The earliest machines were simple devices such as levers, wedges, and wheels. Even the inclined plane, or ramp, is a machine. The task of hoisting a heavy stone block up the side of a pyramid one vertical step at a time, for example, would be made much easier by distributing the slope across an incline. The ancient Egyptians used ramps to build their towering pyramids, an early case of a simple machine at work.

Such straightforward technological principles as levers and wheels have been in use for at least six thousand years. They were a starting point for the ancient Greeks' first automated machines, and they are still used in machines of today. The cogwheel, for instance, is a specialized wheel that has pegs around its circumference, or outer surface. When a cogwheel is set in motion against another cogwheel, its teeth act as levers against the teeth of the second cogwheel and force both wheels to turn in opposite directions. Varying the size of the two wheels can make the second wheel spin either faster or slower. Cogwheels were used in China at least as early as 230 B.C. Greek philosopher Aristotle describes cogwheels in his book *Mechanical Problems*, written about 330 B.C., showing that they were part of ancient Greek technology as well. The gears of modern machinery, such as cars and robots, still use the ancient concept of cogwheels to do things like turn wheels and control the speed and direction of arms or other moving parts. Machine technology constantly builds on earlier discoveries, and developments in the field of robotics are no exception.

The First Automated Inventions

The dream of machines that worked without human help led the Greeks to develop innovative devices powered with energy sources that, like cogwheels, are still used in machines of today: combinations of water pressure (hydraulics), compressed air (pneumatics), wind, and mechanical parts, such as cogwheel-inspired gears. In approximately 2700 B.C., a Greek physicist and inventor named Ctesibius created a pneumatic organ powered by compressed air. He also invented a water pump that was used in automatic fountains of his time and a water clock that he called a clepsydra, a tube filled with slow-draining water that was mostly used to time speeches in the ancient Greek world. According to Nocks, "Ctesibius's clepsydra remained the most accurate clock until the 14th century, when mechanical clocks using a system of loaded weights and levers replaced hydraulic ones."[3] By the time these mechanical clocks were invented in the fourteenth century, the Renaissance was in full swing, a period in which medieval Europeans became interested in reviving the arts and sciences of ancient thinkers. During the Renaissance, European inventors renewed their interest

Da Vinci's Mechanical Man Is Finally Born

In the early 1990s, five centuries after Leonardo da Vinci sketched out blueprints for a mechanical knight, American roboticist Mark E. Rosheim picked up where the Renaissance thinker left off. After collecting as many of da Vinci's rare drawings as he could find, Rosheim followed da Vinci's scheme to create computerized versions of the design for a mechanical man. Rosheim then constructed a physical reproduction of the robot, using stainless steel to fashion the bones and powering the joints with linear electrical motors (da Vinci's drawings featured cables and pulleys). The robot da Vinci envisioned has now come to life, at least mechanically. It can wave its arms, turn its head, and move its jaw. It took five hundred years, but da Vinci's project is finally complete.

in the ideas of automated machinery, and some of their inventions brought science a few steps closer to constructing humanlike robots that worked.

One of the most influential thinkers of the Renaissance was Leonardo da Vinci. Best known as an artist, he was also a scientist and inventor who had studied human anatomy. In 1495 da Vinci drew a set of detailed blueprints (architectural building plans) for constructing a mechanical knight, complete with armor and a helmet, that was probably meant to stand in a castle and entertain visitors. Da Vinci's sketches and diagrams showed technologically advanced joints that would allow the head, jaw, and arms to move. The diagrams for da Vinci's mechanical knight lacked only the technology for powering the joints. "Sufficient prime movers to provide the ideal locomotion Leonardo needed for his machine were still centuries in the future,"[4] says Mark E. Rosheim, a mechanical engineer who holds more than twenty patents in robot technology. Da Vinci's idea of a mechanical man, although very advanced for its time, was more artistic than practical. Rosheim says it followed the pattern of most Renaissance technology in that "emphasis was on artistic and intellectual pursuits rather than applying technology to ease man's burden."[5] Da Vinci's idea was more of an interesting oddity than something society really needed. The social class system of the time provided plenty of servants to do the unpleasant jobs demanded by the wealthy, so there was no real demand for robotic assistants to help with the work. Success in the creation of truly automatic machines, Rosheim says, "would come only when the limits of technology could match the technical and socioeconomic needs of the times."[6] In other words, scientists would need the technology to actually build a mechanical man, and society would have to want one.

The Industrial Age

In the 1800s the structure of European industry began to change, and this led to a society that was much more open to the idea of mechanical workers. For centuries agriculture, which was powered mostly by the labor of humans and large animals, had been the main industry throughout Europe and the newly created United States. By the late 1800s, machines powered by steam and coal brought about a new trend in the working world: the factory. Many people left farms and fields and began working in factories on assembly lines, where each person performed the same task over and over to help assemble tools, textiles, and other items manufactured in large quantities in one location and then shipped to other places. The change from agriculture-based work to mass production of objects and materials was called the Industrial Revolution.

Inventions such as steam power and electricity led to many new technological devices used in factories during this time period, but the new technology also created terrible working conditions. The long days, sweltering rooms, and boring, monotonous hours doing the same thing over and over frustrated the workers. Some factory jobs were also dangerous, especially for the many factory employees who were children or teenagers. Because of their small size, these young workers were often given jobs that required them to squeeze between large machines into tight spaces and close to dangerous moving machinery, the cause of many factory injuries and deaths. It was during the Industrial Revolution that the working class united together and began to use their influence as a group to change and improve their working conditions. If enough employees went on strike and refused to work, factories could not operate, so employers were forced to improve conditions to keep employees content.

By the twentieth century, for the first time in history, society and technology both were ready for the creation of true robots to do human work. The Industrial Revolution had brought about important technological advances in machinery, as well as the means to mass-produce new machines. These discoveries made automated workers a realistic goal. "The industrial revolution that made robots possible also created demands for their use," says Rosheim. As workers became less tolerant of boring or dangerous tasks, he says, "the repetitive, monotonous work that factories introduced created a structured environment ideal for the current generation of robots."[7] By the early 1900s, there was a growing need for machines that could do human work. People began to imagine a world where machines could perform unpleasant human jobs, and these fictional machines became features of popular futuristic stories and plays.

Robots in Science Fiction

The word *robot* was invented in 1920 in a science-fiction play written by novelist and playwright Karel Čapek of Czechoslovakia. The production, called *R.U.R.* (which stands for Rossum's Universal Robots), was about a society in which intelligent machines that looked like humans did boring work for people and even fought wars for them. After a few generations, the machines became intelligent and began having feelings and ideas of their own. They came to resent being controlled by humans. Eventually, the machines took over and began killing the human population. The play serves as a warning for people to think carefully about their creations. While he was writing his play, Čapek did not know what to call his imaginary machines. His brother offered the term *robots* (from the Czech word *robota*, meaning "labor"), and the name stuck. The play opened in Prague, Czechoslovakia, in 1921. It was translated to English and appeared in Europe and the United States in the early 1920s. The word *robots* has been used to describe intelligent, humanlike machines ever since.

When Čapek wrote his play, true robots were still an imaginary invention, but his fearful prediction that robots would one day take over the world never went away. American science-fiction writer Isaac Asimov wrote a number of popular stories about robots in the mid–twentieth century that, like Čapek's play, made many people wary of manmade machines. Asimov's fictional story "Runaround," written in 1942, outlines three laws for the creation of robots. The first law is that robots must never hurt people or, by doing nothing to help them, allow people to be harmed. The second law is that robots must obey human orders, unless those orders are to hurt someone. The third law is that robots must protect themselves, unless doing so disobeys human orders or hurts someone. Although these laws appear in a science-fiction story, they have guided the way scientists and society think and feel about robots ever since. "All science fiction writers after Asimov used the laws as a matter of course," says biographer Michael White. Asimov "somehow knew that one day they would provide the foundation for a set of real laws"[8] about robotics.

Mechanical Tortoises

Asimov was writing fictional robot stories in the 1940s, but there was nothing imaginary about the actual science of robotics that was developing at the same time. A British scientist named W. Grey Walter, who specialized in the workings of the human brain, began to build a number of "thinking machines." The battery-operated machines moved around on three wheels in a tricycle formation, and they were covered with a clear plastic shell that made them resemble tortoises. Walter nicknamed two of his "tortoises" Elmer (a nickname for electro mechanical robot) and Elsie (a nickname for light sensitive, or "ls"), but he also gave them

Developed by neurophysiologist W. Grey Walter, the tortoise machine (pictured without its shell) had sensors that allowed it to respond to light and touch. The machine was among the first to represent what is known as artificial life.

a scientific Latin name, the way biologists name new species of animals. He called his tortoises *Machina speculatrix*: machines that think or speculate.

Elmer and Elsie scanned their environment with photoelectric cells, devices that convert light into electrical energy. These cells served as their eyes. They could detect different brightness levels of light, which in turn powered their motorized wheels. They could head toward light, or if the light was too bright, they could back away from it. They also had contact sensors that could detect bumps and obstacles in their environment, and when they collided with something, they were programmed to change direction. Each robot had a light bulb that turned on when it detected light. The tortoises reacted to the lights of each other and of their own reflections in a mirror in ways that Walter had not programmed them to react. "When Elmer and Elsie would meet," says historian and English professor John Johnston, "both tortoises would enter into a complicated dance," moving closer to each other until their indicator lights were bright enough to make them back away. If one of them encountered a mirror, "its indicator light would flash on and off . . . causing it to 'flicker and jig' at its reflection."[9]

Walter's tortoises were some of the earliest examples of machines that combined thought, action, and interaction with their environment. "Grey Walter believed that intelligence comparable with that found in animals can be created in machines," says Maja J. Matarić, a computer science professor and codirector of the Robotics Research Lab at the University of Southern California. Grey Walter's tortoises, says Matarić, "represent some of the earliest examples of what is now called *artificial life*."[10] The tortoises had their public debut in 1951 at the Festival of Britain, a national celebration of British culture, science, and technology. Only one of Walter's tortoises still exists. It is on display at the Science Museum in London, England.

The First Thinking Robot

W. Grey Walter's tortoises reacted to things their vision sensors "saw" in their environment—namely, light. This was a revolutionary accomplishment at the time. However, by the 1960s, researchers in the field of robotics were interested in building machines that not only sensed things in their environment, but also did things in their environment. These inventors wanted to create machines that could set a goal to do something and make plans for how to do it. In 1970 roboticists at the Stanford Research Institute in Palo Alto, California, finished building Shakey, one of the most famous early robots. Rather than just aimlessly wandering and changing direction when it bumped into things, Shakey actively learned about its environment and could plan its own route across a room.

Like Walter's tortoises, Shakey moved around on wheels. It did not resemble any animal in appearance. It did, however, have thought processes that mimicked the way primitive animals think and plan. Shakey lived in enclosed rooms with white floors and a few large shapes, such as cubes and wedges. The surfaces of these shapes were each painted a different color to help Shakey find its way around. "It carefully

Shakey, pictured with project manager Charles Rosen, was the first robot to actively learn about its environment and perform a primitive thought process.

(and slowly, given the state of computer technology at that time) created plans for which way to move in that special world,"[11] says Matarić. Unexpectedly, it also shook as it moved, which led to its name.

Shakey was an important development in robotics because it paired up two mechanical systems that worked together: the perception system, which takes in signals from the environment, and the actuation system, which acts on those signals. A camera, a range finder, and bump detectors were part of Shakey's perception system. Its actuation system was a computer program used for problem solving and mapping out the environment it sensed. "It navigated from room to room, trying to satisfy a goal given to it," says Rodney A. Brooks, a roboticist and former director of the Artificial Intelligence Laboratory at the Massachusetts Institute of Technology (MIT). "It would, depending on the goal and circumstances, navigate around obstacles, . . . push them out of the way, or push them to some desired location."[12] Shakey only worked in the simple environment created for it, but the robot was a very newsworthy invention at the time. In November 1970, Shakey appeared on the cover of *National Geographic* magazine, and in the same year, *Life Magazine* called it the first electronic person. Shakey is now on display at the Computer History Museum in Mountain View, California.

The First Robots to Navigate

Shakey was an important achievement in robotics because it proved that machines could be designed to move around independently in their environment. However, its potential was somewhat hindered by its poor vision sensors. Shakey was only capable of planning and mapping out a course in a very simple and uncluttered environment created especially for its own limited abilities. In order for robots to be useful in the real world and not just in environments designed especially for them, says Brooks, they must be able to "operate in worlds where the layouts of obstacles are not known ahead of time . . . the sorts of worlds that people and animals can negotiate with ease."[13] Shakey's limited, visual-processing system would have been overwhelmed by "ordinary sorts of environments," Brooks says, places like "cluttered offices with things stuck on walls and disorderly piles of papers that partially obscured objects."[14]

In the late 1970s, two robots were invented that could navigate in complicated environments. Both were equipped with video cameras that they used to view their surroundings and map out the best path from place to place. One of these robots, called HILARE, was invented at the French National Center for Scientific Research in Toulouse, France, in 1977, and the vision technology it used was so advanced that it was studied for decades by researchers in the field of robotics. HILARE's counterpart in the United States was called CART, invented in 1977 by graduate students at Stanford University's Artificial Intelligence Laboratory in Stanford, California. CART was literally a cart attached to

Tomorrow's Roboticists

Every year, thousands of kids and teenagers with a passion for robots meet and compete in a worldwide robot contest called FIRST, which stands for First Inspiration and Recognition of Science and Technology. Since the program's initial competition in 1992, more than 196,000 students and 16,000 robots from around the world have battled for awards and a share of millions of dollars in college scholarship money.

With separate leagues open to kids from six years old through high school, the program sponsors local and regional robotics competitions leading up to the annual world championship. Teams work with professional engineers to design and build a robot, raise funds for their project, and brand and market their finished design, just like real-world roboticists do. Anyone can start a FIRST team with three to ten students in one of the age brackets (kindergarten to third grade, fourth to eighth grade or high school), plus one adult coach.

The First Inspiration and Recognition of Science and Technology (FIRST) contest allows kids from age six through high school to develop robots and compete for scholarships and awards.

bicycle wheels, but it was equipped with its own TV system and a computer for processing the images its video cameras recorded. Like Shakey, CART was able to plan routes, but it could do so in a cluttered environment. It became the first robot to navigate in a natural outdoor landscape. Matarić says that CART, like Shakey, moved slowly "because of the difficulty of processing data from vision cameras and the slowness of computer processing in those days."[15] Also, much like Shakey before them, CART and HILARE were rather useless as anything other than research milestones. The first real, working robot had already been invented, and by the 1970s it was meeting society's decades-old demand for a change in the way factories operated.

A Working Robot

While roboticists were busy inventing robots like Shakey and CART that did intelligent things in the name of research and scientific advancement, industrial inventors of the mid-1900s wanted to build and sell robots that were helpful and profitable, especially in the unpleasant factory environments that had long created problems in the labor force. In 1956 an engineer named Joseph F. Engelberger teamed up with businessman and inventor George C. Devol to create the world's first robot company, Unimation Inc. in Danbury, Connecticut. They then developed and built the first industrial robot, one that could be produced in large numbers to perform tasks typically done by factory employees. Engelberger and Devol's robot was really just a mechanical arm that could be programmed to do specific tasks, but it was perfectly suited

The first industrial robot, Unimate, was well suited for the monotonous work of an assembly line.

for the monotonous and often unpleasant work of a factory assembly line. It was called Unimate, short for universal automation, and in 1961, the 4,000-pound (1,814kg) robotic arm found its first job at a New Jersey plant of the car manufacturer General Motors, where it took a place on the assembly line.

Unimate had two fingers at the end of its mechanical arm that could grasp something as fragile as an egg or hoist steel parts that weighed hundreds of pounds. The robot could be programmed to obey commands that had up to two hundred steps, and when it was needed for a different purpose, it was easy to reprogram. Its first jobs were to take die castings from machines and to weld auto bodies. According to an article in the August 1962 issue of *Popular Science* magazine, Unimate was "designed for five years of two-shift operation without a major overhaul" and demanded "no lunch, no sparing from heavy tasks, no retirement benefits." Where Unimate excelled was "precisely at tasks that human beings shouldn't be doing . . . jobs that are hot, noisy, hazardous, or monotonous."[16]

The earliest Unimate robotic arms cost twenty-five thousand dollars, but companies that bought them for use in factories actually saved money by letting the robots replace human workers, usually at the tasks factory employees hated most. In promoting his invention in 1962 Engelberger said, "Let our mechanical slaves release men from drudgery."[17] Unimate has sold well ever since it was introduced, and it is still being produced today. It is among the world's most widely used industrial robots. As the first example of a robotic invention that met human needs, Unimate was named to Carnegie Mellon University's Robot Hall of Fame in 2003.

Function and Form

Unimate revolutionized factory operations and demonstrated an important idea in the science of robotics: A robot does not need to resemble a complete human being in order

BITS & BYTES

16%

Share of the world's industrial robots in use in North America (compared to 50 percent in Asia)

to do a job. Unimate's single arm and two-fingered hand were perfectly suited for factory work, even though it did not have parts that resembled a human head, torso, or two legs. Unimate's simple but practical design shows that successful robots are created when roboticists closely match the robot's form to its intended job or function. How well a robot works is more important than what it looks like. Humanlike figures may have been a starting point in ancient dreams of independent machines, but in today's robots, form and design are dictated by a robot's purpose.

CHAPTER 2

How Robots Move

Robots are machines that move independently and respond to their surroundings, much the way animals and people do. Leonardo da Vinci's design for a mechanical knight, for example, was closely modeled after the structure of the human body and the way a human being moves. Da Vinci had studied human anatomy, or body structure, in detail in order to create realistic-looking people in his paintings, and his drawings of the mechanical knight showed artificial parts closely resembling the human muscles and joints that work together to move the body. Da Vinci's blueprints "featured the similarity of man to machine,"[18] says roboticist Mark E. Rosheim. Da Vinci may not have built an actual robotic person, but he did tap into one of the core ideas in the field of robotics: He looked at existing biological structures, such as muscles and joints, to model a robotic man.

Patterning robots, or portions of robots, after living things often gives roboticists ideas for how to design them. Roboticist Paul E. Sandin defines robots as "vehicles that move around by themselves and actually do things autonomously."[19] Autonomous means independent, or able to act without help. Like living organisms, true robots operate completely on their own. To create them, roboticists usually do the same thing da Vinci did: They take hints from physiology, the physical and mechanical function of living things, to simulate bodies, limbs, and muscles in their machines. "Robots are not built," says electrical engineer Charles Bergren. "They are born."[20]

A Robot Body

The world is full of living things that move around on their own, and animals are designed perfectly for the environments they live in and the tasks they must carry out to survive. Their size, shape, and method of movement match their environment and biological purpose. Ants live on land, for example, so they have legs that enable them to walk. When roboticists decide on a design for a new robot, they consider where the robot will work and what it will do, and they often copy biological examples like insect legs to plan the robot's body shape and movements accordingly. "Anatomy and kinesiology [the structure and movement of living things] provide guidelines for robot designers,"[21] says Rosheim. Just as animals are shaped by their purpose and role in nature, he says, "robots are being shaped by application or tasks."[22] Few robots are made to look and work exactly like real living organisms, however. Machines do not have muscles, limbs, or energy systems like those in animals. All of their parts must be manufactured out of nonorganic materials, such as metal. Constructing a robot out of nonliving tissue that eventually will move and work by itself like living organisms do is very challenging.

The starting point of building any robot is its body shape, and the more complicated the design, the harder the robot is to build. Therefore, most robot designs start out with a rather basic structure. Then roboticists only add the features and abilities the robot absolutely needs. "We have a working control system very early in the piece," says Rodney A. Brooks, a roboticist and former director of the Artificial Intelligence Laboratory at the Massachusetts Institute of Technology (MIT). In other words, the robot's basic structure and design, including size, shape, and method of locomotion, are in place from the start of the project. "Additional layers [features and abilities] can be added later," Brooks says, but "the initial working system need never be changed."[23]

Most importantly robots need to have a shape that will not get in the way of the job they are being designed to do. Roboticists discovered this after decades of trial and error. Sandin says roboticists used to just "build a chassis, add drive wheels, steering wheels, a power source (usually batteries) . . . and presto! A robot!"[24] Unfortunately, unless the chassis—or body—is well suited for the robot's environment, "the designer will find the robot getting stuck on innocuous objects or bumps, held captive under a chair or fallen tree trunk, incapable of doing anything useful,"[25] says Sandin. Like animals, robots tend to be more efficient and to get stuck less often when they are streamlined. Just as square shapes rarely occur in nature, mobile robots with square edges are uncommon. "A round or rounded shape is easier to maneuver," says Sandin. "The round shape allows the vehicle to turn in place even if it is against a tree trunk or a wall. This ability does not exist for vehicles that are nonround."[26]

In addition to shape, a robot's size and weight are important factors in the design of its chassis, and the roboticist keeps both in mind when considering where the machine will go and what it is being built to do. The early days of robot design allowed robots, such as Shakey and CART, to be whatever size or shape their working parts required, but modern robots are often designed to fit into tight spaces, such as pipes or tunnels, and their bodies cannot be too large or too heavy to do the work for which they are designed. Most robots also have moving parts, such as wheels, arms, or legs, so a robot's size and shape must not be too awkward or heavy for it to move the limbs or wheels that let it do its job.

Robot Limbs and Joints

Not all robots move from place to place, but even robots designed to sit or stand in one place and do the same type of task over and over usually have jointed mechanical arms

Becoming a Roboticist

Job Description: Roboticists design and build robots, discover new uses for existing robots, and conduct research on new technologies in the field of robotics. Most roboticists work at least forty hours a week in an office or laboratory or at a manufacturing plant.

Education: A four-year degree in mechanical engineering, electrical engineering, or computer science is the minimum education required. Many employers prefer to hire roboticists with a master's or doctorate degree in their field.

Qualifications: Employers seek candidates who have professional experience in robotics or have completed a work-study or internship program. Candidates must be creative people who like to solve problems, have excellent computer and technology skills, and collaborate well with others.

Additional Information: Roboticists are in high demand, especially in industries such as manufacturing and the military. The number of job opportunities in this field is expected to rise steadily over the next decade.

Salary: $50,000 to $60,000 per year

that branch off the chassis. The chassis must be the right size and shape for the job a robot is being created to do, but it also must leave room for the robot's working parts. Jointed limbs, such as arms and legs, are the components that most closely resemble the parts of living creatures. Like the arms and legs of humans and animals, robot limbs have joints, places where the limb can bend and move. The more directions a robot limb can move, the more capable it is to carry out complicated tasks. Roboticists follow examples from human and animal physiology to design how a robot's joints will bend and the number of different directions, or degrees of freedom, in which they can rotate.

A joint that moves a limb only one direction, such as forward and backward, has one degree of freedom. A joint that moves forward and backward and side to side has two degrees of freedom. One that moves forward and backward, side to side, and up and down has three degrees of freedom. The most advanced joints, such as the human hip's ball-and-socket joint, also rotate and roll, giving such joints a complete range of motion in any direction with six degrees of freedom. According to Maja J. Matarić, a computer science professor and codirector of the Robotics Research Lab at the University of Southern California, "how many degrees of freedom a robot has is important in determining how it can impact its world, and therefore if, and how well, it can accomplish its task."[27] A robotic arm, for example, will be most useful if it has a number of different joints that, similar to a human arm with its shoulder, elbow, wrist, and fingers, can move in almost any direction to perform complex tasks.

Multiple degrees of freedom come at a cost in robotic joints, however. The more joints a robot has, the more difficult it is to build, to power, and ultimately, to program for the work it will do. Joints are also weak places on a limb. Each joint is made of two pieces of material that are joined together in a way that allows them to bend, twist, or rotate against each other. This flexibility makes the joint suscep- *The presence of* tible to damage or breakage. The more degrees of freedom *multiple joints* joints have, the more directions they can move and the more *in robots causes* flexible they have to be. More flexibility makes joints more *increased flexibility,* fragile. This is one reason the arms of machines, such as *which makes joints* backhoes and cranes, have joints that each tend to move in *more susceptible to* just one direction—back and forth, up and down, or side *damage.*

to side. Because their joints have fewer degrees of freedom, these machines can carry heavy loads without damaging a delicate joint.

Because complex joints take more time to build and more energy to operate, roboticists usually build robots with joints that have the fewest degrees of freedom necessary for the robot's arm or leg to do its job. Few robots have as much mobility as most of the world's animals do. Many robots are even built without the walking ability provided by jointed legs. "Every single land animal uses jointed limbs or squirms for locomotion," says Sandin. "Why aren't there more walking robots? It turns out that making a walking robot is more difficult than making a wheeled or tracked one."[28] Jointed legs each must have their own mechanism for moving, and all the legs of a robot must be fashioned to work together for movement and balance. Track systems, made from two or more wheels connected by a rubber or metal belt that rotates around them (like on an army tank), are easier to operate and provide more stable movement for the robot than legs. Wheels may be easier still. Thus, most robots get around on tracks or wheels. A robot like Unimate, whose job does not require moving from place to place, may even be stationary and bolted to a floor or counter.

For most environments, wheels or tracks are an effective way for a robot to move around. In some environments, however, wheels or tracks can hinder movement and may not be the most practical choice. Wheels can get stuck against large rocks or other obstacles, for example, or they could lose traction in sand. For robots that work in rough and rugged terrain, the ability to walk and climb over difficult obstacles may be worth the extra time and effort it takes to build legs and the extra energy and programming required for them to work properly.

Examples from walking creatures help roboticists create legged machines. A six-legged, insectlike design is often the most practical for walking robots. Unlike a top-heavy, two-legged robot that can easily lose its footing and tip over, or a four-legged robot that moves only one slow step at a time in order to keep the three other legs on the ground for stability, six-legged robots move much the way insects do, always keeping a stable tripod formation of three legs on the ground—two on one side, one on the other—while the other three legs lift and move forward. Insects have one of the most stable and efficient leg designs on Earth. When Brooks and two other scientists at MIT set out to build a walking robot named Genghis in 1988, they chose a similar six-legged design. The result was an efficient walker that looked like a mechanical bug. "At no point did we intentionally make the robot insect-like in its appearance," says Brooks, "but it certainly ended up that way."[29] Although robots with six legs, like Genghis, look peculiar, they can easily climb stairs and get past other obstacles, such as rocks, that could stop a wheeled robot. The six-legged structure has become a popular and reliable robot design.

One drawback of having multiple legs is that in robots, just as in animals, every limb must be powered by something that puts force on it to push and pull it back and forth at the joint. In animals, this force is created by muscles. In robots, it must be simulated by actuators, the mechanisms that act as

The insect-like robot Genghis, pictured, was made with multiple joints and legs. The more legs a robot has, the more complicated the design becomes.

Animals as Models

When it comes to getting around, robots lag far behind animals that can swim, fly, scamper, sprint, slither, and climb, but the science of biomimetics (literally, the miming of living things) is helping robots catch up. Many robotic critters now move like the animals that were their models. At MIT, for example, RoboSnail gets around on a thin layer of slime, like the snails that inspired it. Researchers at Carnegie Mellon University built a robot that walks on water, copying basilisks, lizards that slap their feet to do the same thing. At Stanford University, StickyBot looks and works like a mechanical gecko to scale slick surfaces, such as glass, while Sprawlita darts around at speeds of several meters per second, fast enough to give its inspiration, the cockroach, a run for its money. The springy Jollbot at the University of Bath in the United Kingdom flings itself into the air like a grasshopper, and MIT researchers have built waterproof, robotic fish designed to swim in schools. Made with the newest materials and technology, biomimetic robots are almost as well suited to survive in the real world as the living animals that inspired them.

Machines, like the robotic fish pictured, are being built to mimic animalistic movement.

a robot's muscles. Because each joint needs an actuator, the more arms, legs, and joints a robot has, the more actuators it needs, and the heavier, bulkier, and more complicated its design becomes.

Robot Muscles

For robots to get around, roboticists must manufacture the artificial muscles that move them. Organic muscles are made of filament—long, fibrous sections of tissue that contract and relax to shorten or lengthen a muscle. The ends of the muscles are attached to bones at either side of a joint.

For example, in people, the bicep muscle is attached to the humerus bone in the upper arm and to the radius bone below the elbow. When the muscle contracts, or shortens, it pulls the radius toward the humerus. When the muscle relaxes, the radius swings away. Often, the muscles of living things work in pairs, one muscle contracting and the other relaxing in an alternating pattern that lets bones move forward and backward smoothly at their joints.

In the field of robotics, the actuators, or manufactured muscles, provide the leverage the robot needs for movement. The three most common types of actuators are pneumatic,

Actuators act as a muscle for a robot by releasing stored energy that causes its limbs or wheels to move.

A ROBOT'S MUSCLE

The biceps muscle is attached to the humerus bone in the upper arm and to the radius bone below the elbow. When the muscle contracts, or shortens, it pulls the radius toward the humerus. When the muscle relaxes, the radius swings away. This same action is accomplished in robots through the use of actuators.

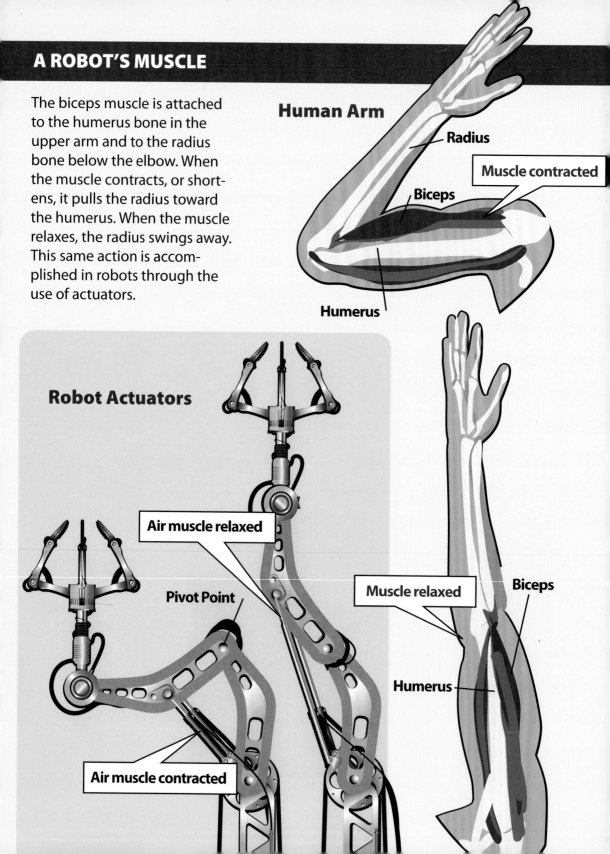

Human Arm

Radius

Muscle contracted

Biceps

Humerus

Robot Actuators

Air muscle relaxed

Pivot Point

Air muscle contracted

Muscle relaxed

Biceps

Humerus

hydraulic, and electric. Pneumatic actuators are powered by air pressure. Hydraulic actuators are powered by pressurized fluids. Electric actuators are powered by electrical charges and magnetic forces.

Although there are different designs for pneumatic and hydraulic actuators, the general design for both types is a chamber that is filled with either fluid or air. A valve controls the amount of fluid or air inside the chamber, and thus, the valve controls the pressure. As the fluid or air pressure builds up, it creates a force that pushes a small platform in the chamber down against a spring. When the valve is opened and air or fluid escapes, the spring pushes the platform back to its starting position, releasing stored energy in the spring. This energy in turn can make a robot's arm or leg move back and forth (a linear actuator), or can spin a robot's wheel (a rotary actuator).

The third type of robot actuator is an electric motor, the most common actuator in robot design. A motor uses magnets, which have positive and negative electrical poles, or ends. Opposite poles attract each other, and similar poles repel each other. Thus, a positively charged electrical end of one magnet will be drawn to the negatively charged end of another, whereas two positive or two negative poles will push each other away. Electrical forces that constantly attract or repel each other create a circular, or rotational, movement in a motor, because the ends of the magnets are pulling and pushing against each other. When opposite electrical forces are contained in a small space (such as a motor) and cannot move away from each other, they spin instead, creating a constant circular motion. An electric actuator (motor) can be hooked up to an axle, which in turn drives the wheel it is connected to into a spin. An axle might also be hooked up to a cogwheel set against another cogwheel. When the first cogwheel turns, it puts force on the other cogwheel to turn the opposite direction. This gear mechanism, frequently used to move a robot's parts, is usually powered by an electric actuator.

All three types of actuators can be effective ways to put pressure on robot arms, legs, tracks, or wheels to make the robot move. All three actuators have limitations, too. For example, pneumatic and hydraulic actuators tend to be large compared to the size of the robot, because they need chambers large enough to build up sufficient air or fluid pressure to move the robot's parts. The size of pneumatic and hydraulic actuators makes a robot heavy, and if a robot's arm or leg needs to move in opposite directions—both forward and backward, for example—then each joint might need two actuators, one that pulls and one that pushes, the way human muscles work together. This will make the robot even heavier.

One way around this problem is the pneumatic artificial muscle (PAM), an actuator that, like a balloon, fills with air and then expands or shrinks the way organic muscles do. The PAM accomplishes both tasks of a muscle: contracting and relaxing to move a limb back and forth at its joint. But the PAM, like any hydraulic or pneumatic actuator, has the potential for another problem: leaks. A loss of pressure due to a leak in a hydraulic or pneumatic system means the actuator will stop working correctly. In a hydraulic system, a leak not only means a malfunctioning actuator but also a messy spill of a fluid, such as oil, that could damage other parts of the robot.

Electric actuators are often the most practical type for robots because they tend to be smaller and less bulky than pneumatic or hydraulic actuators. They also are not as prone to malfunctioning because of leaks. A limitation of electric actuators, however, is that they usually turn best at one speed. A remote-control car, for example, will surge forward at the press of a button, and when the button is released, the wheels stop turning and the car stops. This all-or-nothing type of actuator is not ideal for robot parts that require changes in speed or levels of pressure, such as an arm that must be able to pick up heavy objects, like tools, and fragile ones, like eggs. An electric motor can make an actuator difficult to control when smaller movements or slower speeds are necessary. Pneumatic and hydraulic actuators, on the other hand, can create a precise amount of pressure to move the robot as much or as little as needed. They usually are also stronger actuators, so arms and joints that do both precise work and heavy lifting may function best if they are built with pneumatic or hydraulic actuators as their muscles. Because they are bulky and require chambers to hold air or fluid, "hydraulic and pneumatic systems are rather difficult to implement effectively," say electronics experts Gordon McComb and Myke Predko; however, "they provide an extra measure of power"[30] compared to electric motors.

Robot Energy

Whether a robot's actuators are pneumatic, hydraulic, or electric, they need energy to function and make the robot move. Muscles of living organisms require energy, too, but they are powered by body cells that make energy from the food the animal eats. This energy is released by the cells to do the body's work and make the animal move. Robots do

Batteries are the most common source of robot energy, powering the machine with an electrical charge.

not have the ability to make their own energy from food, so to make their actuators turn wheels or move arms and legs back and forth, roboticists must build in some method of providing energy to the robot and its parts.

Batteries are the most common source of robot power. A battery is a device that converts chemicals into an electric charge. When wired to an actuator, the battery sends an electric current along the wires to make the actuator's parts work: The charge will make an electric motor spin to turn a wheel, for instance, or will make a pneumatic or hydraulic valve move to create pressure and build energy that is then used to move a robot's parts. "Batteries are an integral part of robot design," say McComb and Predko. "To robots, batteries are lifeblood; without them robots cease to function."[31]

There are many different types of batteries, from the standard alkaline batteries used to power flashlights, toys, and household products to much more expensive and complex batteries such as the lithium-ion type used to power laptop computers. Lithium-ion batteries are small, lightweight, and work for a long time before needing to be recharged, but they are also one of the most expensive batteries on the market, and they may not provide enough energy for robots that consume huge amounts of power. Other types of batteries, such as nickel-cadmium batteries, may cost less than lithium-ion batteries, but they can be heavy and bulky, especially if a robot has many actuators, each requiring separate battery power. Still other battery types, such as lead-acid batteries used in cars, are unpopular in today's robot designs because of the danger of leaks and the problem of disposing of used batteries that are harmful to the environment.

When choosing a robot's battery, roboticists consider how much power (and how many batteries) the robot needs, the weight and bulk of the batteries, the length of time the batteries will operate before needing to be replaced or recharged, and the overall cost of running the robot with battery power. Because some types of batteries are prone to leaks, safety for the robot and for the environment is another concern. Ultimately, the robot must have enough battery power to

Segway Transporters

In 2002 the Segway company began selling personal transporters, two-wheeled scooterlike appliances. People ride them by standing on the platform between the wheels and holding on to handlebars. They are controlled and steered by the rider leaning forward, backward, or side to side. A quiet motor, the strength to carry heavy loads, and long-lived batteries with an onboard charging system make Segway technology ideal for robots, too. The Segway Robotic Mobility Platform is fast becoming the wheel system of choice for roboticists who want fast, reliable transportation over rugged terrain. Because Segway balances itself and recharges on its own, the technology frees up memory and power for all the other things a robot is meant to do. Roboticists can now build their robot, then attach it to a hardy Segway platform and send it out into the world. One invention using Segway is a robot designed to fight forest fires. Charging over rough terrain at speeds up to 28 miles per hour (45kmh) while carrying up to 400 pounds (181kg) and equipped with a hose that blasts out 10 gallons (38l) of water per second, the Segway-inspired robot can replace up to three humans during a forest fire. Segway technology like this is a vast improvement for wheeled transport systems.

do its job without being too large, clumsy, or heavy, without running out of energy unexpectedly in the middle of an important task, and without costing too much to build. Powering a robot is one of the biggest challenges in robot design. It is also one of the aspects of robotics in which new technology is having the most impact.

New Types of Robot Batteries

Roboticists are constantly seeking new and better ways to give robots needed energy. After all, a goal of robotics is to create completely autonomous machines. "Autonomous means acting completely independent of any human input,"[32] says Sandin, and this includes human help to detect when batteries are running low and to change or recharge them. Solar-powered batteries are one example of a power source that recharges itself. They use the sun's energy to power photovoltaic cells, devices that convert light into energy. However, these batteries are still extremely inefficient. Technology journalist Gareth Branwyn says, "Only a small percentage of the energy that reaches a cell is actually absorbed and converted into electrical current."[33] Nevertheless, solar power is seen as a possible way for robots to recharge their own batteries, especially robots that are designed for use in space.

Other robots are being designed with fuel cells, devices that use hydrogen and oxygen—two elements in endless supply on Earth—to create the electrical current that drives a valve or a motor. Smaller and lighter than most batteries, fuel cells are also easily recharged anywhere as long as hydrogen and oxygen are in supply; batteries, on the other hand, must be hooked up to a power source in order to be recharged. Fuel cells are expensive, however, and are not well suited for robots working in very hot or cold environments, since fuel cell designers have not yet created models that function well at extreme temperatures.

Still other roboticists are experimenting with technology that allows robots to make their own energy by digesting sources of food. Such robots follow the example set by animals: They identify food sources, such as plants, ingest them, and break down the materials to release energy in a process similar to animal digestion. The EATR is a robot being constructed by Robotic Technologies Inc., a commercial robot design and consulting company based in Maryland. Intended to provide support to the military during long wartime missions, the EATR is expected to generate enough power from eating 12 pounds (5.4kg) of plant material to drive between 2 and 8 miles (3.2km to 13km). "We expect to have a prototype EATR vehicle by April 2011," says Robert Finkelstein, president of Robotic Technologies. "An operational system could be available by 2012 or 2013."[34]

The EATR is another example of how roboticists continually study living creatures, not only to design the bodies and moving parts of their robots but to find new ways to power their inventions. The physical design and capabilities of a robot make up only the first half of its development, however. Once a roboticist has chosen the right body size and shape; added the wheels, tracks, arms, or legs a robot will need; and chosen the best way to power the robot's moving parts, another equally important task remains: adding a mechanical brain that will transform the robot into a fully functional, working machine, one that can think for itself.

CHAPTER 3

How Robots Think

Even a brilliantly designed robot is worthless without an equally brilliant brain that is capable of guiding the robot through the lifelike tasks its body was built to do. Maja J. Matarić, a computer science professor and codirector of the Robotics Research Lab at the University of Southern California, notes another way that animals and robots are similar: "Both need a brain to function properly."[35] Brains do so many things in living creatures that it is impossible to survive without one. The brain detects information from the environment and processes it so the animal understands what is happening nearby. Even more importantly, the brain makes instant decisions about what to do with environmental information, forcing the animal into action to move toward the things it wants or to get away from danger. A brain also has the ability to learn—it remembers what the animal senses in the environment and stores the information so the animal can perform the same response when it encounters something a second time.

Even simple brains of simple creatures like cockroaches process and store information to help the cockroach carry out tasks of life. The brains of more advanced animals, especially humans, carry out incredibly complicated tasks, such as communicating, feeling emotion, solving problems, being creative, and making judgments about things, processes that neuroscientists who study the brain and its effects on the body do not yet fully understand. Unlike muscles and joints, whose design and function can be studied just by looking at them, a brain's complicated workings are not readily apparent. Nonetheless, if roboticists are to build machines that move and act as though they are alive, they must also build brains that are up to the challenge. "Without a brain of some type and the ability to respond to different environmental information," say electronics experts Gordon McComb and Myke Predko, "a robot is really nothing more than just a motorized toy."[36]

BITS & BYTES

25%
Proportion of the Microsoft Corporation's research budget that is spent on artificial intelligence projects

Machines that process information and react to it are called computers, and the same kind of technology that exists in every laptop or desktop computer can be adapted for a robot to help its body move in the ways the roboticist intended. "An almost endless variety of computers can be used as a robot's brain,"[37] say McComb and Predko, and changing technology is constantly making these computers more capable, responsive, and intelligent. The computer chips that constitute a robot's brain must be programmed to do the tasks the robot is built for, but the things computer scientists can program a robot to do are growing more complex all the time. Robots are becoming an increasing part of the human world, and by building capable computerized brains, roboticists are making robots smart. They are giving them artificial intelligence.

Manufacturing a Brain

"The science of Artificial Intelligence (AI) might be defined as the construction of intelligent systems," says physicist and computer scientist Marcus Hutter. A system, he explains, "is anything that has an input and an output stream," and intelligence "can have many faces like creativity, solving problems, . . . surviving in an environment, language processing, knowledge and many more."[38] Thus, the goal of artificial intelligence is to build a system that receives input—cues and information

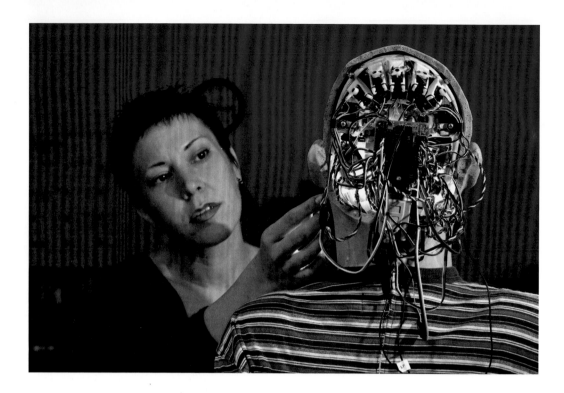

Scientists must program robot brains to use the perceptive connections that humans make when processing information from the five senses.

from its environment—and responds with some sort of reaction, or output. A computer, for example, receives input from a keyboard and from a mouse. The computer processes these signals to respond in some way, such as by printing a document or playing a movie.

In robots, the computerized brain must be programmed to handle specific kinds of input and to do different things with that information. Usually, a robot's output will serve to move it in some way as it reacts to input. "The nature of the programming depends on what the robot does," say McComb and Predko. "If the robot is meant to play tennis, then its programming is designed to help it recognize tennis balls, move in all lateral directions, perform a classic backhand, and maybe jump over the fence when it wins."[39] Just as a robot's body structure must be built for the jobs or tasks it does, a robot's brain must be built to sense certain things in the environment so that the robot can react to them properly in order to complete its job. Even before a robot does something, or produces output, it must gain input from its environment, the same way people and animals do with

The First Robotherapist

The ability to carry on a conversation is difficult for robots, because real discussions require creative thinking they cannot perform. In 1966 a computer scientist named Joseph Weizenbaum seemingly solved the problem with a computerized psychotherapist robot named ELIZA. A patient could type in a problem or a question, and ELIZA would display a relevant response on its screen. Conversations were carried out about anything the patient wanted to discuss. ELIZA mimicked a real therapy session by answering questions with questions or rewording the patient's thoughts. For instance, "I feel sad" might be answered with "Why do you feel sad?" When ELIZA did not know how to respond, it said general things like "I see," or "Tell me more."

ELIZA did not really think. It was merely programmed to respond in certain ways. Still, its patients often finished therapy sessions feeling better about their problems. The technology behind ELIZA lives on. It is used in Web support platforms that ask users to type questions about subjects they need help with. Voice recognition technology has brought the same concept to computerized telephone operators who give responses such as "I can help you with that." Artificial intelligence has led to believable, if artificial, conversation.

their eyes and ears and the nerves of their skin, all of which are connected to the brain by way of nerves in the central nervous system. Robots need some sort of central nervous system, too, connected to its brain by wires. A computerized brain must have a computerized way to sense the environment before it can be programmed to react to it.

Robot Sensors

Roboticists are interested in equipping their mechanical inventions with some of the same senses people have. People have five senses they use to receive information about the world: sight, hearing, touch, taste, and smell. Each sense requires different tasks from the brain. The human brain processes and reacts to things the eyes see, for example, differently than to things the body hears, smells, tastes, or touches. An artificial brain also needs to perceive, categorize, and make sense of things in its environment, but sensory

Most robots are equipped with sensors that, at a minimum, give them sight, touch, and hearing capabilities.

perception takes up power and space. Roboticists conserve both by equipping robots to sense and process only the most necessary details, those that will help them carry out essential tasks. At a minimum, most robots need to be able to see, feel, and hear in order to avoid danger and prevent themselves from running into things as they move and work. Thus, most robots have some kind of sensory system that gives them sight, touch, and hearing.

Even early robots, such as Shakey and William Grey Walter's tortoises, had a way to see. They had video cameras so they could record images of what was in front of them. Their computers processed these two-dimensional images, and the robots responded with output behaviors, either moving toward objects or moving away from them. Some early robots also had vibration sensors to help them detect when they had bumped into something so they could back up and head in a different direction. When Rodney A. Brooks, a roboticist and former director of the Artificial Intelligence Laboratory at the Massachusetts Institute of Technology (MIT),

ECHOLOCATION

Researchers continue to develop sensory technologies that help robots to perceive distances. Often these advances are inspired by nature. Some robots, for example, are built to judge the distance to nearby objects by sending out sonic pulses and tracking how long it takes for these sounds to echo off of things and return to the robot. This process, called echolocation, lets a robot gauge distances much the way bats sense their environment through sound. It is the same process that enables bats to hunt for insects even in total darkness.

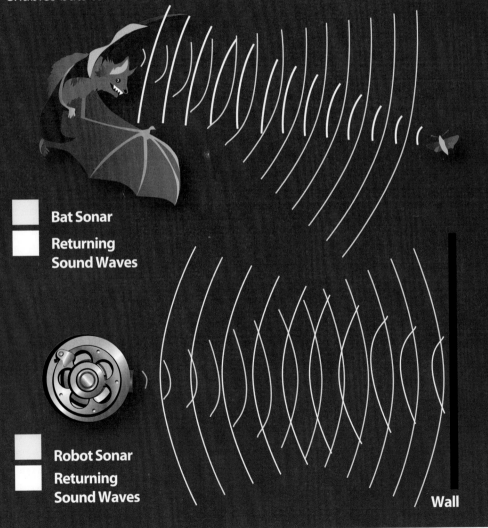

Bat Sonar

Returning
Sound Waves

Robot Sonar

Returning
Sound Waves

Wall

and his colleagues created their six-legged walking robot Genghis, they invented a sensory device it could use to prevent bumping into things at all. "In order to anticipate obstacles better, rather than waiting until the front legs are rammed against them," says Brooks, "each of two whiskers is monitored by a *feeler* machine."[40] Such primitive sensory devices worked well enough for what those first robots were designed to do—basically roll or walk around and try not to crash into things. But as robots evolved into machines designed to carry out more specific, useful, and complicated tasks, their sensory methods had to evolve, too.

One sensory limitation of early robots was their two-dimensional vision. They were able to identify light patterns and images in front of them, but only in a flat plane. They had no depth perception, the way people do. The human eye can see in three dimensions, telling the brain not only that there is an object ahead, but also how far away it is. Human eyes also see color and can detect movement, and they have peripheral vision, meaning they can see motion coming in from the periphery, or outer edges, of their field of vision. People see motion from the top, bottom, or sides even when their eyes are focused on something straight ahead. For a robot to operate well in a human world, it needs vision sensors that can handle similar tasks.

Modern robots are built with camera vision that can do all of these things. There are robots that capture images in three dimensions and in color, detect movements, and perceive distances, just as people can. Researchers have developed other sensory technologies, too: There are robots that detect differences in temperature, sense bumps and other movements in the world around them, and even judge the distance to nearby objects by sending out sonic pulses and tracking how long it takes for the pulses to echo off the objects and return to the robot. This process, called echolocation, lets a robot gauge distances much the same way bats sense their environment and hunt for insects even in total darkness.

These sensory developments help roboticists create machines that do much more than just move to avoid obstacles. Robots are now capable of detecting many of the same signals from the environment that people can, and even some that

Robots Deal Out Losses

In 1997 IBM's software program Deep Blue made history when it beat world champion chess player Garry Kasparov at his own game. The event proved that computers finally could outthink people, processing possible chess moves and outcomes with lightning speed. The game of poker is another story, however. The card game requires a great deal of psychology, not just strategic moves. Poker players are allowed to bluff, or mislead, about the cards they are holding, and computers, so far, cannot do this. In a 2008 Texas hold'em poker game between two professional poker players and a computer software program called Polaris 2.0, the humans won—although not by very much. As computers get smarter and maybe even start to have emotions, the day may come when robots will sit around poker tables with human players and bluff with the best of them.

people cannot, such as trembles and motions in the ground that are too slight to be felt by people. But even as sensory perception is improved, roboticists face the challenge of linking what the robot can sense with what the robot can do with the information. The input-output system not only requires robots to perceive the world, but also to understand these perceptions and act on them. "An effortless glance reveals the pieces on the chessboard," says roboticist Hans P. Moravec, "but it takes long, hard thought to plan good chess moves."[41] How robots respond to the information their sensory systems take in is just as important as the senses themselves. It is also one of the most complicated aspects of artificial intelligence. People themselves do not fully understand how humans can think and reason, but roboticists must program such functions into the computerized brain of a machine. Robots must not only see and move the chess pieces, but also actually play the game with strategy.

Robotic Reasoning

The kind of autonomous, independent behavior roboticists want their creations to display involves perceiving something specific, then knowing what to do with the information.

Robots need to use the details they sense about their environment in order to create a mental map of their surroundings. They are designed to see obstacles in their path and to plan a way around them—not just any way, but the fastest and easiest way. Modern robots use information from the environment to reason and make choices. They can store information in their brains. They can remember and learn. They have artificial intelligence.

Learning Artificially

One of the problems roboticists have always struggled with is the fact that robots need to survive in an unpredictable world, even though their programmed behavior is entirely predictable. Early robot programmers had to anticipate and program a response for every sort of obstacle or situation a robot might encounter, or its computerized brain would not

An artist's rendering of the concept of artificial intelligence. Roboticists are researching ways to allow computers to "think" like a human brain.

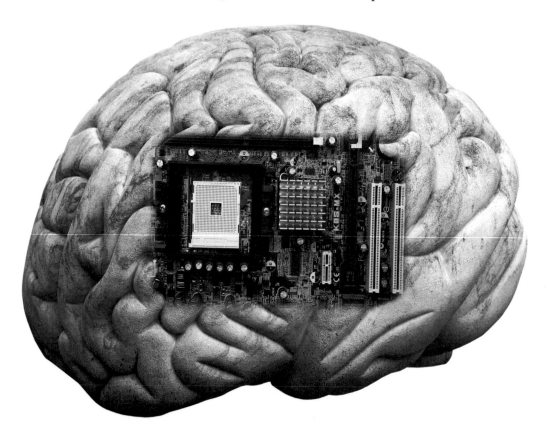

know how to react. The world people actually live in is impossible to completely predict. The outcome of a football game, for example, is anyone's guess, since every action and consequence that could happen in the game cannot possibly be foretold. Human behavior, like the way football players react to circumstances in a game, is spontaneous and requires judgment and reasoning.

People themselves often do not know what they would do in a certain situation until they are in that situation. Programming such complicated thinking processes into a robot's computerized brain is far more difficult than just programming codes for behaviors the robot should carry out when certain things happen to it. "The most interesting behavior happens between the extremes of order and chaos, when responsive mechanisms dance with complicated environments," says Moravec. "In a rich environment," he says, an ideal robot's behavior "would intertwine spontaneity with rule-following, just like a human being."[42] This is where the future of robotics is headed, but artificial intelligence is not yet this advanced. One way roboticists are getting around the limitations of not-quite-human brains is by programming robots to communicate with humans who can tell them what to do.

Connecting Robot and Human Minds

Today robot bodies are being built with almost human capabilities, such as the National Aeronautics and Space Administration's (NASA) Robonaut, a robotic astronaut that looks and works much like a person from the waist up. Designed to help human astronauts work on the International Space Station, Robonaut has the vision and body structure to carry out many of the same complicated tasks that a human astronaut can do. Robonaut is not only nimble but also extremely intelligent, in robot terms. Its computerized brain coordinates all the movements of its many

RoboPups

In the early 1990s, the Sony Corporation invented one of the world's first and best-known robopets: a robotic dog named AIBO. The robot's plastic body had four jointed legs, a wagging tail, and a computerized brain that learned to recognize its owner's voice and could be programmed to do tricks. Capable of many things living dogs can do, including fetching newspapers and greeting family members at the door, AIBO had many benefits of a real pet but none of the nuisances. It did not require food, it did not need to be housetrained, and it caused no allergic reactions in humans. For a while, AIBO seemed the wave of the future, but in 1996, Sony stopped making the toy, naming a poor sales record as the reason. These plastic partners apparently lacked the warmth and fuzziness that people enjoy with real dogs.

Sony developed the robotic dog AIBO. The mechanical pet is complete with jointed legs, a computerized brain, and even a wagging tail.

complicated joints, allows it to understand and obey human commands, and even reacts appropriately when part of its body malfunctions. Nevertheless, complex brain functions like reasoning, problem solving, and making good decisions if it encounters an unforeseen problem are beyond Robonaut's capabilities.

Scientists have found a way to give Robonaut humanlike insight by linking its computerized brain with that of a human astronaut through teleoperation, the control of a machine from a distance. Teleoperation was made possible by the same advancements in communication technology that gave rise to wireless networking. In the case of NASA's

Robonaut, a human operator is linked to the mechanical astronaut by a complex system of video camera technology, audio transmissions, and remote-controlled gloves that link the sensory experiences of Robonaut in an outdoors space environment with those of a human controller sitting inside the space vessel, some distance away. The things Robonaut "sees" with its camera vision are transmitted to the human operator, who wears a helmet outfitted with screens that display the images the robot is taking in. The operator also wears gloves that communicate with the robot's hands by way of a real-time computer operating system. Robonaut responds to everything the human operator does. If the operator moves her head to look up, sensors in the human operator's helmet transmit signals to Robonaut to do the same thing, and Robonaut's cameras in turn transmit the view to the operator. If the operator moves her gloved hands—for instance, to mimic the motion of tightening a bolt—signals are sent to make Robonaut's hands do that precise movement, too. Robonaut even hears and responds to the operator's verbal commands, and it can recognize certain objects so that the

NASA developed Robonaut, a robot with almost human capabilities, to help work on the International Space Station.

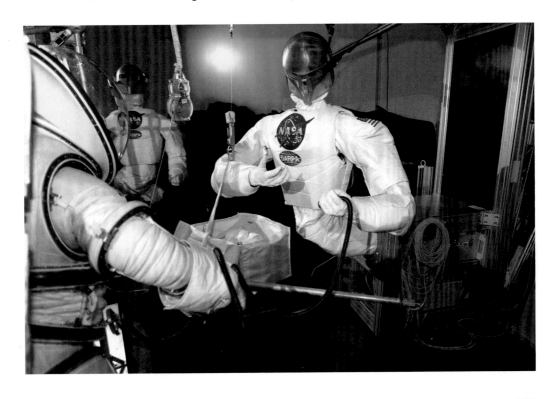

NASA's Robonaut

Inside a white, padded astronaut suit designed to cushion it from collisions with space debris, NASA's space android, Robonaut, looks and moves almost exactly like a human. Each of its hands has the same joints and parts as a human hand, along with fourteen motors and twelve separate circuit boards. Robonaut's shoulders, elbows, and wrist joints have sixteen sensors each, along with sensitive brake systems. Robonaut's joints use special lubricants and are leak proof to prevent anything from seeping out of Robonaut into a space shuttle's zero-gravity environment.

All the materials used to make Robonaut are resistant to extreme temperatures. It has skin made of synthetic fabric for added insulation. Its aluminum endoskeleton tapers off into a stub at the waist, which Robonaut uses to balance itself and change position. The head has cameras that simulate human vision and can see color, depth, and peripheral movement. Robonaut even wears a helmet to protect its cameras from floating debris.

operator can simply give a command such as "pick up the wrench," and Robonaut will obey.

Such advanced teleoperation makes a vital connection between robot bodies and human minds that can think and feel and reason, tasks computer science has not yet been able to program into robot brains. But it is getting close. "Our goal is to achieve human-like motion, intelligence, and communication," says Robert Ambrose, a leading scientist for the Robonaut project at NASA. "Initially, we imparted these skills to Robonaut via teleoperation...however, we continue to develop new software and sensors to enable shared control and, ultimately, autonomy."[43] Robonaut's future descendents may indeed be capable of thinking and reasoning to do jobs in space without any human intervention at all. Teleoperation is one of the first steps to accomplishing this landmark in robotics, because it combines a robot's physical abilities with the thinking ability of the human brain. Robonaut can already act independently some of the time, such as disobeying its human operator if it realizes the directions it has been given would cause it to crash into something or damage itself. This is a step toward giving robots the same self-awareness people have about the condition of their own body and what is good for it. This kind of knowledge is essential for robots to be able to operate on their own in the world.

Robot Self-Awareness

The ability of a robot to sense what is happening in its own body is as important as programming it to sense its environment. Unless it is aware of what is going on within itself, a robot cannot determine when it is damaged, for example, or when something inside of it has malfunctioned, or even when it is tipping over and needs to move to regain its balance. Humans and animals are highly aware of their own physical state. They feel hunger and thirst when they need nourishment; they feel pain when something has injured them; they get tired when they have exercised too hard or need sleep; and they can sense when their bodies are off balance, reacting to prevent or soften a fall. Animals are also equipped with instincts, such as fear that makes them run from danger. Human beings, the most self-aware of all the earth's creatures, have emotions like love and affection for people they like. For a robot to truly resemble humans, it needs to have the same kind of self-awareness, or proprioception, that humans have. "Without an awareness of its own configuration," say Josh Joseph and Brandon Luders, graduate students in MIT's Department of Aeronautics and Astronautics, "a robot has no way to distinguish itself from its environment, resulting in undesirable and unpredictable behavior." Proprioception, which Joseph and Luders say is now "widely regarded as one of the primary human senses, along with sight, sound, taste, smell, touch, and balance,"[44] is an important goal for the development of artificial intelligence if robots are to tend to their own needs and protect themselves without the help of humans.

"In practice, most robot systems are designed to have the proprioception necessary to estimate and control their own physical state," say roboticist Henrik I. Christensen and computer scientist Gregory D. Hager. "Recovering the state of the world from sensor data is usually a much larger and more complex problem."[45] This is because the robot's body systems and abilities are known by the roboticist. Unlike the environment outside of the robot, in which every condition or situation can never be known at the time of programming, the robot's brain can be programmed to know its own size, shape, and weight, how it moves, whether it has tipped over, and even if its batteries need to be recharged. Just the same, programming self-awareness into robots is challenging, because the roboticist not only considers what the robot should know about itself, but what it does with that information. Sensing that its batteries are running low, for example, is most useful if the robot knows how to recharge its batteries or how and where to obtain fresh batteries and install them. Knowing that some of its parts have been damaged or are not working properly is most useful for the robot when it can fix itself. Otherwise, the robot can only signal to a human operator that it is not working right. It is not fully independent.

Many modern robots are capable of both sensing their own bodies and fixing some of their problems themselves. A personal robot called Cye, invented by Probotics Inc. in 1999, can be programmed to do household jobs, such as carrying dishes and retrieving mail from a mailbox, and is one example of a robot whose batteries never run out midtask. When it registers that its batteries are running low, Cye is programmed to find its own recharging station and reenergize itself.

Another new breed of robots, called self-configuring modular robots, can actually put themselves back together if different sections become separated. "They have the potential to perform self-diagnosis and repair," say roboticists Mark Moll and Daniela Rus. The robots, made up of separate sections called modules that work both independently and together as a whole, can "identify what the global arrangement of modules should be and what each individual module's role is"[46] if the robot's parts become separated, such as by crashing and tumbling. Robots that have the self-awareness to recharge themselves when their batteries get low and even to fix themselves when their parts are damaged have abilities that will suit them for living completely on their own, without any human help at all. This will be an increasingly important quality as robots are built to do more and more tasks that human beings either cannot do or do not want to do. Robots that have the intelligence and proprioception to work without any human intervention at all will greatly increase their own worth and will push the science of robotics into ever more advanced uses.

CHAPTER 4

How Robots Are Used

Today's robots are designed to do jobs and to go places that are unpleasant, dangerous, or even impossible for humans. The more they are made to function and interact in a human world, the more lifelike robots behave, and people are beginning to recognize certain qualities of living things in them. As roboticists invent robots that are ever more intelligent and advanced, people can talk to them and even play with them. They are becoming mechanical companions.

As Domestic Companions

Robots have the potential to make ideal household companions for people. A favorite character in the futuristic 1960s cartoon *The Jetsons* is Rosie, an apron-wearing robotic maid whose square body and face are the only nonhuman characteristics she possesses. Rosie cooks, cleans, and gives plenty of intelligent, motherly advice to her human family. Although just a cartoon character, Rosie is a popular example of how robots might one day step in to do housework and free people from their boring chores at home. In the decades since Rosie was created, the percentage of American families in which both parents work full time has more than

Robot Champs

The Darmstadt Dribblers of Germany was the winner of the 2009 RoboCup, an international soccer tournament for robots. In its team photo, the four-player German team looks like a hodgepodge of mismatched klunkers, but on the field, they are a force to be reckoned with. Their superior teamwork and decision-making and ball-handling skills lead to goal after goal. The Dribblers use a wireless local area network (LAN) connection to know the positions of everyone on the team, and their cameras recognize field lines, goals, and the moving ball. They can walk or run. If they fall, they can get up again. They do it all without any human help whatsoever, because those are the rules of the RoboCup games. The annual tech tournament, which began in Japan in 1997, now features three thousand robots from forty countries, separated into leagues by size and body type. RoboCup is one of the most important events of the year in robotics and artificial intelligence. Stay tuned, World Cup: Roboticists predict that by 2050, robots will compete against human soccer teams—and win.

RoboCup, a robotic soccer tournament, is one of the most important events of the year in the artificial intelligence community.

doubled, rising to about 70 percent in 2005, according to the U.S. Census Bureau. Busy schedules leave far less time for housework, but only about 9 percent of working families pay housekeepers to clean for them. The rest find time to maintain their own homes. The field of robotics is stepping up to meet an increasing demand for help with household tasks among busy American families.

A company called iRobot, founded in 1990, manufactures a line of affordable robots that do various household jobs that many people hate to do. One of the company's best-known products is the Roomba, a small, flat, plate-shaped robot that moves autonomously to vacuum every inch of the floor in a room. "It ranges around the room partly at

The Roomba robot uses navigation technology to vacuum floor surfaces while sensing walls and other obstacles.

random, covering open areas in widening spirals, then carefully following walls when it finds them, lightly bouncing off the occasional lamp or chair leg," writes reporter Lev Grossman in a 2002 *Time* magazine article about the Roomba's debut. Grossman also writes, "When Roomba determines . . . that it has covered every part of the room several times over, it stops, beeps cheerfully and shuts itself down."[47] Millions of Roomba robots have been sold since the device's debut in 2002. Owners of these automated vacuum cleaners now can have their floors cleaned while they spend time on other things.

Other products offered by iRobot are Scooba, a floor-mopping robot; Dirt Dog, which sweeps the floors of shops and garages; Verro, a robot that scrubs swimming pools; and Looj, which cleans tree leaves and other debris out of a house's gutters. The Roomba and its sibling robots come in different sizes, models, and price ranges for home and business use. The most basic model of Roomba costs about a hundred dollars.

Getting Dirty Jobs Done

There are no robots yet that do other household chores, like dusting furniture and scrubbing toilets, but robots already help keep houses clean in another important way. They are being used to make sure that household drains keep draining. If the drains and toilets of every home and building in a city or town became clogged and started to back up, the smell and mess would be dreadful.

Sink and shower drains and flushing toilets are connected to ductwork and pipes buried underground. A sewer, the

The Roomba by iRobot

The robotic vacuum cleaner Roomba has a plastic chassis that features a carrying handle, an on-off switch, and buttons for vacuuming an entire room or just one spot. Roomba's underside reveals the parts of a standard vacuum: two front rollers that sweep dirt up from the floor, a main cleaning deck that uses suction to pull dirt into the vacuum inlet, and a bin to collect the dirt. Five motors power Roomba's rollers and treaded wheels. To turn, it powers just one wheel.

On the front of Roomba's chassis is an infrared sensor that detects walls, furniture, and other obstacles, so Roomba can slow down and turn before it crashes. There are also sensors on its bumper to alert it of a collision. On its underside, Roomba has two cliff sensors that prevent it from tumbling down stairs. Roomba's belly holds its rechargeable battery pack and two self-charger contacts. Some Roomba models use an infrared signal to find and dock into their own battery-recharging unit. An onboard microprocessor receives data from the sensors to memorize the size and layout of a room. All an owner has to do is turn Roomba on.

collection site for all the liquid human waste produced in an urban area, is connected to homes and businesses by sewer pipes that create an underground network collecting liquid waste from every drain and toilet in town. Sewer pipelines can be miles long, and maintaining the system is not the most pleasant of jobs for people. "Checking sewers for leaks, cracks and blockages is a task most of us wouldn't touch with a bargepole," writes journalist Justin Mullins in an article in *NewScientist* magazine. "An engineer will normally inspect a sewer, or alternatively, send a remote-controlled video camera trundling through it and watch the pictures above ground. Either way, it's time consuming and unpleasant."[48]

Nonetheless, sewer lines do develop problems, and it is up to people to fix them. Most of the world's cities have sewer pipes that are several decades to more than a century old. Some of the older pipes are made of clay that is now cracking; other pipes are joined together at their seams by mortar that has deteriorated. Most sewer lines are buried under roads, buildings, and houses, so digging down to the pipes to repair them is not always an option. Scientists and city officials are

Robots like "Sam," pictured with technicians Randy McLemore and Chris Fields, are being used to navigate sewer pipes to fix problems.

instead fixing sewer-line problems with robots called pipe crawlers that are designed to fit inside sewer pipes, locate leaks and blockages, and even fix cracks. One example is a German-made robot called KARO, short for KanalRoboter (which means "sewer robot" in German). KARO uses cameras to record and transmit images from inside a sewer pipe to human operators on the outside. It also uses microwave sensors, which generate electromagnetic waves that can penetrate sewer-pipe surfaces and move into the surrounding soil. These waves move farther in dry soil than wet soil, so the microwave sensors allow KARO to determine wet areas outside the sewer pipe, a sign that the pipe may have a leak. KARO is connected to the entrance of the sewer pipe by a tether, in case the robot gets stuck or stops working and needs to be pulled out.

Other sewer robots, such as the Pipe Rover, can operate without tethers. Originally designed to look for leaks and blockages in the sewers of Hong Kong, China, the Pipe Rover communicates with its human operators by ultrasonic waves. It can roll along on its treaded track system in flat-bottomed pipes or stand up on legs if pipes are round or slippery. In a large city like Hong Kong, which covers 425 square miles (1,101sq. km) and is home to almost 7 million people, robotic sewer scouts do a more thorough and cost effective job of pipe inspection and repair than humans could do alone. "Combined data from multiple [robot] sensors allow for accurate determination of debris locations," according to a 2009 article in *Trenchless International* magazine. "This, in turn, would allow the city to direct sewer cleaning operations to those specific locations as opposed to cleaning the entire sewer, saving significant time and money."[49]

The technology of pipe-crawling robots is not limited to sewer systems. Any pipe system or ductwork, such as oil and gas pipelines or air-conditioning ductwork in skyscrapers and other huge buildings, can benefit from robotic pipe explorers. "In the last decades, different applications have been envisioned for these robots," say electrical engineers Manuel F. Silva and José A. Tenreiro Machado, "mainly in the technical inspection, maintenance and failure or breakdown diagnosis in dangerous environments."[50] The nuclear industry is one such dangerous environment that now uses robots to examine pipe systems carrying radioactive substances. Radiological Services Inc. invented a robot called the Pipe Crawler to perform pipe inspections in nuclear power plants. The Pipe Crawler can operate in pipes as small as 2 inches (5cm) in diameter. It is equipped with sensors that measure radioactive energy and can detect leaks that could be deadly to human inspectors. Independent, crawling robots are now central to safety in the nuclear industry.

Robot Batteries

Sluggish batteries hold robots back. The more complex a robot, the sooner its battery power is drained. Larger batteries let a robot work longer before needing a recharge, but too much battery weight makes a robot bulky and impractical. Bigger batteries might help the Roomba vacuum last longer, for instance, but they also would make it too fat to squeeze under furniture and too heavy for people to lug up stairs.

Better batteries are on the way. Researchers at the Massachusetts Institute of Technology are making a lithium-ion battery that recharges in seconds, not hours. Lithium-ion batteries contain ions, electrically charged particles that increase a battery's overall charge as they circulate through it. The faster the ions circulate, the more charge they create and the faster the battery reboots. The new technology involves coating lithium ions with a slick, glassy covering that gives them amazing speed. The new and improved lithium-ion battery could recharge a cell phone or a laptop computer in the time it takes to brush one's teeth, or recharge an electric car in the time it takes to eat lunch.

Exploring Dangerous Environments

Radioactive areas, such as manmade nuclear reactors, are only one example of dangerous environments where robots are working for humans. Machines are also taking over jobs in some of the world's most hazardous natural environments, where it is difficult and unsafe for people to venture. A robot called the SnoMote, for example, explores the frozen glaciers of Greenland and Antarctica to collect data on the mass of the glacial ice sheets. Environmental scientists need this information to determine whether the polar glaciers are melting, and if so, how fast. "Given the substantial impact these structures can have on future sea levels, improved monitoring of the ice sheet mass balance is of vital concern,"[51] says Derrick Lampkin, an assistant professor in the Department of Geography at Pennsylvania State University and one of the scientists working with the Georgia Institute of Technology to build SnoMotes.

The giant sheets of polar ice will determine the water levels of the world's oceans in the next few decades. The ice

New robotic techniques allow scientists to conduct research in dangerous environments. Robots like Dante II, pictured, gather information and samples from unsafe terrain such as volcanoes.

caps are slowly melting because of global warming, and as a result, oceans will swell, affecting the world's shorelines and the habitats of ocean wildlife. However, with average yearly temperatures as low as −13°F (−25°C), these regions are very inhospitable for humans to study in person.

SnoMotes are autonomous robots that can work without human help to explore an assigned area or region of a polar glacier. They use cameras and sensors to move around, and they take measurements of ice density and thickness that environmental scientists use to determine if, and how quickly, the ice caps are melting. Several SnoMotes are designed to work together as a team, communicating with each other to cover all the ground scientists assign to them. With the help of these robots, scientists need not expose themselves to the deadly glacial cold.

EXPLORING ROBOTS DIVE DEEP

In 2009 Nereus, the world's deepest-diving robot, became the first device to explore the Mariana Trench since 1998. The trench, located in the Pacific Ocean near Guam, is the deepest abyss on Earth. Nereus descended into the Mariana Trench with 25 miles of coiled tether, which allowed it to stay connected to researchers during the search.

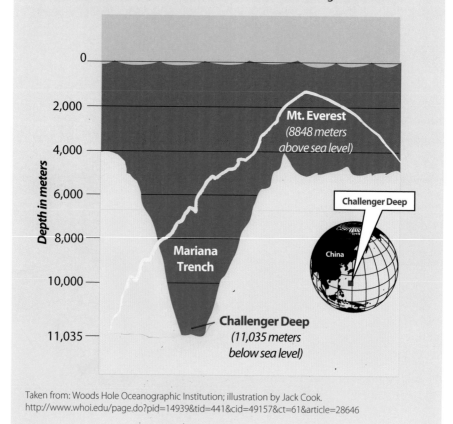

Taken from: Woods Hole Oceanographic Institution; illustration by Jack Cook.
http://www.whoi.edu/page.do?pid=14939&tid=441&cid=49157&ct=61&article=28646

Environments of excessive heat are as threatening to human life and well-being as frozen glaciers are, so scientists studying active volcanoes are making use of robots as well. Not only are active volcanoes sources of intense heat, but they also spew deadly gases, making the area difficult for humans to study safely. To get closer to active volcanoes, gather samples of toxic gases, and collect important volcano data, researchers from the National Aeronautics and Space Administration (NASA) and the Robotics Institute at Carnegie Mellon University in Pittsburgh, Pennsylvania, developed a robot called Dante II in the early 1990s and tested it in the Alaskan volcano Mount Spurr in 1994. With the help of a tether, the six-legged robot crawled down the steep and uneven side of the volcano's crater to gather gases and take measurements inside the volcano. According to the institute's Web site, robotic explorers such as Dante II open "a new era in field techniques by enabling scientists to remotely conduct research and exploration" in volcanoes and also to explore "extreme (i.e., harsh, barren, steep) terrains such as those found on planetary surfaces."[52] With the aid of robots like Dante II, scientists hope to eventually be able to predict when a volcano will erupt so people living nearby can be warned.

Other robots explore volcanoes in even more challenging circumstances than the slippery slopes and steaming chasms of land volcanoes. A robot named ISIS, for example, was completed in 2006 to explore volcanic eruptions and other geological phenomena that take place on the ocean floor. Roboticists at Durham University in Great Britain have sent ISIS, a robotic submarine the size of a van, 3 miles (4.8km) beneath the surface of the ocean to explore active volcanoes at the bottom of the sea. ISIS also has traversed an undersea chasm off the coast of Portugal that is the size of Arizona's Grand Canyon. "In a control room like something out of Star Wars, a team 'flies' the robot down into the dark,"[53] writes David Shukman in an article for CDNN (Cyber Dive News

800,000

Approximate number of people who will be needed to work in the robotics industry until at least the year 2016, according to the U.S. Bureau of Labor Statistics

Network). High-definition cameras and rock-collecting arms on the ISIS allow scientists to see, retrieve, and study things in regions of the ocean that are too deep for human beings to explore safely. "Researchers are for the first time able to view previously hidden features up to 5km (3 miles) deep,"[54] according to Shukman.

ISIS is not the only robot to achieve impressive underwater feats. In May 2009, a submarine robot named Nereus took a dive to the deepest known place in any of Earth's oceans: the Mariana Trench, located in the Pacific Ocean near the island of Guam. Shaped something like a sled, Nereus can be programmed to operate autonomously or can be connected to a human control center with a thin fiber-optic tether. Nereus carried 25 miles (40km) of coiled tether into the Mariana Trench and uncoiled the necessary amount as it descended so that it remained connected to researchers on the surface throughout the expedition. When it descended into the Challenger Deep, the deepest part of the Mariana Trench and the deepest known ocean crevice in the world, Nereus reached a depth of 7 miles (11km)—more than

Mission to Mars

July 4, 1997, was an important date for planet Earth and its galactic neighbor, Mars. It was the day the Mars Pathfinder lander set down on the Martian surface, seven months after being launched from Earth. Its robotic passenger, the rover Sojourner, disembarked to begin its mission of driving around, taking pictures, collecting data on rocks and climate, and transmitting everything back to Earth using radio waves. Sojourner's working life lasted twelve times longer than its creators had hoped. In the eighty-three days before it stopped working, the robotic geologist took 550 pictures, performed fifteen chemical assays of Martian rocks and soil, and sent back millions of information tidbits, indicating, among other things, that Mars was once a warm, wet planet. With no way to return to Earth, Sojourner is now stranded somewhere in the northern hemisphere of Mars, but it has other robots for company, such as the NASA explorers Spirit and Opportunity that landed on Mars in 2004. Scientists believe a human trip to the red planet is also on the horizon, perhaps as soon as the year 2020.

2 miles (3.2km) deeper than the height of Mount Everest, the world's tallest mountain. Water pressure at that depth is about eleven hundred times the pressure on the ocean's surface and would crush a human being.

Robots alone make it possible for people to see what exists at such depths. "With a robot like Nereus, we can now explore virtually anywhere in the ocean," says Andy Bowen, Nereus's project manager and lead developer at the Woods Hole Oceanographic Institution in Woods Hole, Massachusetts. "I believe it marks the start of a new era in ocean exploration."[55]

Exploring perilous environments, such as glaciers, volcanoes, and ocean trenches, no longer requires the physical presence of humans. By building robots with enough artificial intelligence to maneuver in these spaces, take pictures, and gather materials and data, people can explore never-before-seen areas without exposing themselves to danger.

Keeping Us Safe from Explosives

Robots are also being built to protect people from manmade dangers, such as bombs. Since terrorists crashed airliners into the World Trade Center in New York, the Pentagon in Virginia, and a field in Pennsylvania on September 11, 2001, the United States has been on the lookout for bombs hidden on planes, trains, buses, and other forms of public transportation. Terrorist attacks like the one that took place on commuter trains in Madrid, Spain, in 2004, in which terrorists used hidden bombs to kill 191 people, have made better bomb detection and removal an important goal for public safety.

Robots are now doing this job in many airports and public transportation areas. One robot, called teleMax, can enter airplanes, trains, and buses to search for and disable small, lightweight bombs hidden in luggage compartments. TeleMax moves on a system of four treaded tracks that operate well even on stairs and steep ramps. Its body is narrow enough to fit down the aisles between plane, train, and bus seats, and it has a telescoping neck that can stretch up to 8.5 feet (2.6m) to search overhead

Robots are being used to detect, mark, and even disable landmines and other explosives.

luggage bins. The robot communicates with a human operator working a safe distance away. The operator gives teleMax instructions for using its built-in tools to disable and remove hidden bombs.

According to Kuchera Engineering, the company that makes teleMax, a bomb disposal engineer who uses the robot "saves precious time by more easily negotiating complicated routes to suspicious objects."[56] Robots like teleMAX make bomb detection and deactivation safer for humans who do this job, and it could save thousands of lives by finding and disabling bombs planted by terrorists on public transportation.

Robots are also being used to detect and mark deadly landmines, bombs that are buried in the ground and are designed to explode when a person walks on it or when a vehicle drives over it. Millions of landmines have been planted in battlefields since World War II. The United Nations estimates that more than 110 million unexploded landmines are buried in sixty-eight countries. Landmines kill or injure as many as two thousand people in the world every month.

In response to this problem, roboticists are working to invent machines that can detect underground landmines and mark their locations. In 2004 a group of engineering students at Johns Hopkins University in Baltimore, Maryland, invented a lightweight robot, made mostly of plastic, that uses metal detectors and camera imaging to find possible landmines buried in areas of thick vegetation.

The remote-controlled robot transmits a picture of a suspected landmine to its human operators, who then direct it to mark the spot with a squirt of spray paint. Humans can then walk into the area safely to find and dig out the landmines. Carl V. Nelson, a physicist and researcher in Johns Hopkins University's Department of Mechanical Engineering, says the robot can "get off the road, off the clear paths and go into rougher terrain like bushes and high grass, where mine detection would be difficult to do by hand."[57] Robots like this one make the dangerous but important job of finding and removing landmines much easier and safer for people and help prevent thousands of deaths from landmine explosions.

Robots on the Battlefield

A major area of research in the field of robotics is the creation of machines that can perform dangerous tasks during war. Roboticists at the Lawrence Livermore National Laboratory in Livermore, California, for example, invented the Tethered Scout Robot, a remote-controlled device that soldiers can steer over rough terrain. The robot can carry or tow a weight of at least 10 pounds (4.5kg) as far as 1,000 feet (305m) from its human operator, so that soldiers can move small equipment or supplies back and forth across open spaces without exposing themselves to danger.

Roboticists also have invented more advanced, autonomous scouting robots. The United States Marine Corps Warfighting Laboratory (MCWL) in Quantico, Virginia, for example, builds a military robot called the Dragon Runner, a four-wheeled device that soldiers can throw off the back of a moving vehicle or over a wall or fence. The Dragon Runner can land upside down or right side up; it works just as well either way. After it lands, it independently begins scouting an area and relaying information to soldiers using a video camera, a microphone, illuminated sensors for night vision, and infrared (heat-detecting) sensors that help it identify and avoid obstacles as it gathers details about an enemy environment.

The U.S. military also uses unmanned ground vehicles (UGVs), such as the Gladiator, a robot that looks like a miniature army tank equipped with camera sensors and a machine gun. The Gladiator is teleoperated by a soldier and performs scouting and surveillance missions, and if necessary, shoots at potential threats to nearby U.S. soldiers.

The U.S. military is even developing medical robots to help soldiers who are wounded on the battlefield. Roboticists have invented a Trauma Pod, a portable, enclosed chamber where a wounded soldier rests while a two-armed robotic surgeon within the pod telecommunicates with a human physician

Technology has allowed the creation of robots that move ahead of military troops to scan the area for bombs and landmines.

some distance away to assess the soldier's injuries and perform emergency medical procedures, such as inserting a breathing tube, giving antibiotics and painkillers, and cauterizing (heat-searing) wounds to stop heavy bleeding. "The result will be a major step forward in saving lives on the battlefield,"[58] says Scott Seaton, executive director of the Engineering and Systems Division at SRI International, the company that invented the Trauma Pod.

Today's robots scout battlefields for enemies and bombs, engage enemy soldiers in gunfire, and even give wounded soldiers medical treatment. It is clear that robots will have a major role not just in the future of humanity but also in the future of warfare. Someday robots may even stand in for human soldiers to prevent the loss of human life during war. At the same time, robotic soldiers are among the things science-fiction writers have long warned against in their stories. Mechanical soldiers are one of the most controversial aspects of robotic technology among people who worry about the effects, good and bad, that robots may have on the future of humankind. Robots that are built and programmed to kill could become so efficient at the job that they threaten the very safety of humankind if the technology falls into the hands of people who use it for evil purposes—or if robots one day begin to think for themselves and turn against their human creators.

BITS & BYTES

$10 billion

The amount of money the U.S. military spent on unmanned, robotic vehicles in the first decade of the 21st century

CHAPTER 5

A Society Shared by Robots

Mechanical doctors helping fallen soldiers on a battlefield is one of the newest and most promising advances in the field of robotics. The robots working in a Trauma Pod use radio and video camera technology to communicate with human surgeons. Someday robots may be able to diagnose the injuries of wounded soldiers and operate on them without any human help at all.

Some robots are already working in hospitals and doing a better job at delicate surgeries than human doctors do. A company called Intuitive Surgical, for example, has created a surgery station with four robotic arms: one that records high-resolution, three-dimensional camera footage of the patient's surgery site and three that perform every aspect of the surgery, from making incisions to putting in the sutures that close the surgical wound. A human surgeon sits nearby at a console, viewing high-definition footage of the surgery site and controlling the robotic arms that perform the surgery. Intuitive Surgical says the robotic arms are even more precise than human doctors' hands. The surgery station, called the da Vinci Surgical System, is used in major hospitals all over the world and is an example of how far the field of robotics has come since Leonardo da Vinci's fifteenth-century sketches of a mechanical knight.

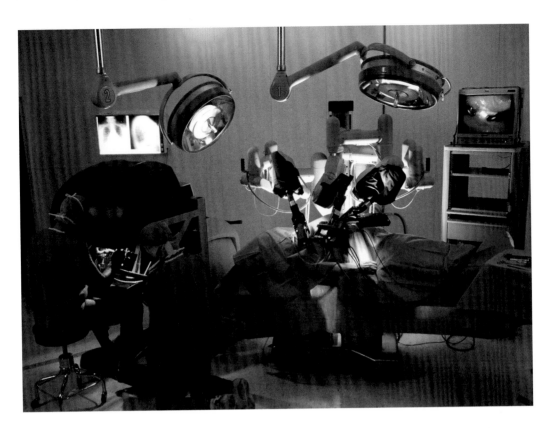

Robots are helping humans with an ever-growing variety of jobs and problems. They assist with medical surgeries and military operations. They explore areas like ocean trenches and volcanic vents. They fix problems in sewer lines. They help astronauts work on the International Space Station. They even vacuum carpets and mop floors. With every passing year, robots do more things that are helpful to people, but even the most advanced robots, such as the da Vinci Surgical System and the NASA Robonaut, still require direction from human controllers. Although more intelligent and skilled than ever before, robots do not solve complicated problems, invent new ideas, possess human emotions, or think entirely for themselves—yet. Computer and robotic sciences continue to evolve at a rapid pace, however. As robots get increasingly smarter and help humankind in countless new ways, they could have the potential to join human beings as a dominant species on Earth, especially if they eventually can think and feel for themselves, which would

The robotic da Vinci Surgical System remotely performs surgery. A human surgeon controls the robotic arms while he views the three-dimensional image of the operation site.

$15 billion

The amount of money the world population is expected to spend by the year 2015 on personal robots, artificial servants that people can program and use at home

lead to making their own decisions and no longer depending on people to tell them what to do.

Emotional Robots

An important area of research in robotics is how to give machines the ability to form the same kind of spontaneous feelings or reactions to things that people have. This is something even the most advanced robots cannot yet do because all their reactions must be preprogrammed. "Robots are, after all, clumps of wire and steel," says theoretical physicist Michio Kaku. "It is emotions which distinguish us from creations of metal."[59] These emotions, or feelings, are complex mental responses to events or situations. Emotions are one of the most important biological advances of the human race, because they guide the behavior and choices not just of individuals but of entire societies.

In part because of their emotional reactions toward each other, humans are very social creatures and have always lived in groups, something that has ensured human survival and development. Belonging to a tribe or a family lets people work together for protection, food, and shelter but also for fun, learning, and companionship. Emotions such as joy and sorrow help people feel affection for one another, something that encourages them to work together to survive. Fear prompts people to recognize danger and protect themselves. Anger and jealousy make humans competitive, always wanting to improve and learn. Curiosity drives them to invent things.

Robots, however, lack the emotions possessed by their human creators; feelings like love, curiosity, and desire that lead to spontaneous reactions. "The kind of social intuition we have is very powerful and probably uses close to the full processing power of our brain—the equivalent of a hundred trillion calculations per second,"[60] says roboticist Hans P. Moravec. Such complicated brainpower is something robots do not yet have, at least not in forms that would make

them personable companions. "Humans are a profoundly social species," say Rodney A. Brooks, a roboticist and former director of the Artificial Intelligence Laboratory at the Massachusetts Institute of Technology (MIT), and Cynthia Breazeal, a roboticist specializing in robots that interact with people. Brooks and Breazeal claim that most of today's interactive robots behave so predictably they come across as uncaring and unsociable, and "as a result, they frustrate us and we quickly dismiss them." Roboticists, they say, "need to address these issues or people will not accept robots into their daily lives"[61] as anything more than machines. Sooner or later robots will be everywhere, says Nilanjan Sarkar, a mechanical and computer engineer at Vanderbilt University in Nashville, Tennessee, and "as they become increasingly common, they will need to interact with humans in a more natural fashion."[62]

Roboticists are responding to the demand for more socially and emotionally capable machines by building robots that have changing moods. These robots do not yet possess the kind of human emotion that will allow them to interact

The robot Kismet can understand human emotions and offer facial responses that convey fear, happiness, and surprise.

with people realistically, but some can now recognize the feelings of people around them and respond in appropriate ways. Researchers at MIT's Personal Robots Group have developed a robot named Kismet, for example, that can see and understand human emotions and respond with appropriate emotions of its own. Kismet's metallic head, thick lips, and piglike ears make it resemble a robotic primate more than a human being, but nonetheless, its face can move in ways that demonstrate surprise, happiness, sorrow, fear, interest, and disgust. Even more important, Kismet knows when to display such behaviors: It looks sad when a person scolds it, for instance, and it looks irritated if its four camera eyes show that people are getting too close to its face. "Facial expressions, body posture, gaze direction, and quality of voice . . . they all contribute to the readability of Kismet's expression and ability to communicate its internal state to a human in a natural and intuitive way,"[63] say Brooks and Breazeal. Importantly, Kismet is not just mimicking human expressions but actually using them to show its needs, such as whether it wants attention or wants to be left alone. Robots that use emotions to get a certain reaction are an important step in creating lifelike machines that could one day interact in the human world, because this is how humans interact with each other.

Researchers at MIT's Personal Robots Group also developed an emotion-sensing robot named Nexi, whose face looks much more human than Kismet's. Made of white plastic, Nexi has a jaw, eyebrows, and eyelids that move in response to its many different moods. Nexi can nod, wink, smile, frown, glare, open its mouth in surprise, and look disgusted. Its built-in eye cameras see and interpret the emotions of the people around it. Not only can Nexi show its own mood to others, as Kismet can do, but it can also learn from the moods of the people around it. According to the Personal Robots Group's Web site, "even learning simple tasks or concepts from human subjects is difficult for robots because of the challenging perceptual problem introduced by the variability and richness of human behavior."[64]

Nexi is one of the first in a new generation of robots that may be able to make sense of what nearby people do and say and whether or not that means they are pleased. "It is difficult to develop robotic systems that people are willing to interact with over an extended period of time," says the Personal Robots Group's Web site. "This work is motivated by our desire to develop social robots that can successfully learn what matters to the average citizen."[65] Named one of *Time* magazine's fifty best inventions of 2008, the charming and interactive Nexi may one day be sociable enough to serve as a companion for the elderly, or even a teacher for young children.

Robots that have humanlike feelings in response to their own needs and the needs of people are close to being truly autonomous, with the ability to think for themselves. Robots with minds of their own, machines that serve not just as

Testing Artificial Intelligence

In 1950 British mathematician Alan Turing developed a test to see how computer intelligence compared to human intelligence. The test involved one computer and two humans: an interrogator who asked questions and a responder who answered them. The interrogator sat in a separate room from the computer and the responder, who were named "X" and "Y." The interrogator did not know which was which. He asked questions of each of them, and at the end of the session, he used their responses to guess which one was the computer. In 1950 computer responses were easy to spot, but Turing predicted that by the end of the twentieth century, computers would be able to fool an interrogator into believing they were human.

The experiment, called the Turing Test, is now used to measure artificial intelligence in an annual competition called the Loebner Prize Competition in Artificial Intelligence. A cash award and a medal go to the makers of the computer that fools the human interrogator most often. So far, Turing's prediction has not come true—computer intelligence is still fairly easy to spot. But some scientists predict that by 2030, a computer will finally pass the Turing Test and be as smart as people.

human servants but as intelligent companions, have long been a dream of humankind, one often seen in movies that feature endearing robotic characters.

Expectations for Robots

"In the minds of many people," says computer scientist George A. Bekey, "the word 'robot' is associated with images of human-like machines with super-human intelligence, strength, or abilities."[66] Filmmakers have a long history of portraying this idea in robotic movie characters. Friendly robot companions have been much-loved cast members in some of history's most successful blockbuster films. The golden-colored android C3PO and his three-wheeled sidekick R2D2, for example, are well-loved characters in George Lucas's *Star Wars* movies. They are memorable big-screen robots that not only think for themselves and solve problems but also display likeable human behaviors, such as loyalty and a sense of humor. The title character of the 2008 Disney Pixar movie *WALL-E* is another robotic character with human characteristics. The rusty, trash-collecting cartoon robot moves around on tracks, recharges his own batteries

The title character of the movie WALL-E represents what some imagine to be the humanistic robots of the future.

with solar panels, and survives on Earth in the complete absence of humans. However, WALL-E shows many human-like emotions through body language, making him loveable to movie audiences. Like humans, WALL-E longs for companionship and acceptance, and he has a sense of right and wrong. He represents what some people imagine to be the humanistic robots of the future.

The clone army in the Star Wars *movies shows the dangers that can occur when technology falls into the wrong hands and is used to control humankind.*

In the real world, intelligent machines have the potential to provide many valuable services and even be companions for humankind. They may become language interpreters, a skill that will be in ever-higher demand as globalization brings different cultures of the world together. Robots also may become restaurant waiters, hotel stewards, and teaching assistants in schools. They could one day fill in for human workers in industries such as health care, which is becoming short staffed as the patient population grows faster than the number of human nurses available to provide care. Future robots might perform patient-care tasks, such as giving medications and helping patients to the bathroom.

As the world's population ages, robots also may become reliable helpers for the elderly by pushing wheelchairs, helping them get dressed, and even chatting with them. Robots might assist people with disabilities, too, perhaps filling the role of Seeing Eye dogs that are trained to help blind people cross streets and get around safely. "The commercial potential in this area is enormous," says Bekey. However, he adds that robots used in person-centered industries such as health care must be virtually fail proof, because mistakes can have deadly consequences. Robot perfection, he says, "is a tall order indeed."[67]

For robots to achieve their full potential in industries such as health care, they eventually will need to have intelligence, judgment, and common sense equal to that of humans. Safety guidelines for early robots like Unimate were limited to preventing them from accidentally smashing or crushing objects or people. As robots become more intelligent and perform more complicated tasks, robot safety will involve not only programming them to avoid the mistakes their human creators predict, but also trusting them to prevent unpredictable accidents and mishaps on their own. "We must be willing to be cradled in the metal arms of our creation," says electrical engineer Charles Bergren. "If we tremble at the thought, we should review our designs."[68]

Giving robots the ability to plan, make choices, and think entirely on their own opens up new and exciting possibilities for robots. It also creates what some people see as a danger. If humans design robots that think for themselves, those robots could one day use their own intelligence against humankind.

Becoming a Robot Technician

Job Description: Robot technicians work for companies that manufacture robots. They install and program new robotic systems for the company's clients and customers. They are also responsible for robot maintenance and repair.

Education: Most robot technicians have a two-year or four-year degree in a technical field, with coursework in hydraulics, pneumatics, electronics, and computer science.

Qualifications: Completion of an apprenticeship or training program with the hiring company is usually required.

Additional Information: Robot technicians are in high demand. They often travel to the customer's location to install, repair, or maintain robots. They also provide telephone and online support to customers. They may help write instruction manuals for the robots their company makes. Some work as independent consultants. Robot technicians sometimes work night shifts or are on call.

Salary: $30,000 to $50,000 per year

This, too, is a recurring theme in popular robot movies. *Star Wars* and *WALL-E* show robots in a positive and lovable way, but both movies also show a darker side of robotic technology. In the *Star Wars* movies, entire armies of robotic warriors are used by evil rulers to patrol and control the universe. In *WALL-E*, the earth's human population lives in space, surrounded by intelligent robots that serve but also control people. "The genius of 'WALL-E,'" says *New York Times* movie reviewer A.O. Scott, "lies in its notion that creativity and self-destruction are sides of the same coin."[69] Movie robots represent both the promise and the danger of human inventiveness. In the real world, roboticists are creating technology that allows robots to have emotions and begin thinking independently, and some people believe such robots could turn against their human creators, like the robot armies that set out to destroy humankind in the 1980s movie *Terminator*.

Robot Ethics

Nowhere is the potential danger of robots greater than on the battlefield. Already remote-controlled robots like the U.S. military's Gladiator are capable of shooting at enemies. A human-controlled battle robot like the Gladiator is dangerous, Bergren says, because "it may fall into the hands of operators with less than good intentions."[70] A completely autonomous battle robot that could make its own decisions about what, where, and when to shoot is even more frightening. Once roboticists build machines that can think on their own, says Bekey, "the consequences are unpredictable, and they could be dangerous for humanity."[71]

The potential for robot technology to fall into the hands of people with evil intentions, or for intelligent robots to form evil intentions on their own, has led to a need for a code of ethics in the field of robotics. Ethics are beliefs about what is good and bad that shape moral decisions and feelings of duty and obligation. Increasingly, as robots become more capable and intelligent, roboticists must consider ways to build into them some sense of right and wrong. "Robots will require an ethical awareness," Bekey says, "to ensure that in pursuit of some goal, they do not perform actions that would be harmful to people or other robots in some unethical way."[72]

Once machines are built that can think on their own, many feel that robots could pose a threat to humanity.

Some countries are even establishing codes of ethics for roboticists. South Korea, one of the world's most technologically advanced countries, has a goal to place a robot in every South Korean household by the year 2020. In 2006 South Korea's government drafted the Robot Ethics Charter to prevent people from abusing robot technology and to prevent the creation of robots that will abuse people.

Some of the charter's ideas are similar to the laws of robotics created by science-fiction writer Isaac Asimov, which state that first and foremost, robots should not harm humans, or by not acting to help humans, allow them to be harmed. These ideas will be increasingly important as truly autonomous robots become a reality in the future. "Robotics is a new science with a manifold of applications that can assist humans and solve many, many problems," says roboticist Gianmarco Veruggio of the School of Robotics in Genoa, Italy. "However, as in every field of science and technology,

Lying, Cheating Robots

In 2008 roboticists at the Swiss Federal Institute of Technology in Zürich, Switzerland, created a group of robots that moved around and could light up to communicate with each other. The roboticists placed "food" in the robots' environment that recharged their batteries and "poison" that drained their batteries. The robots were set loose to learn which sources were food and which were poison. In time, the robots not only distinguished food from poison, but they also lit up to tell others when they found food.

The roboticists had expected their robots to learn to communicate when they found food; the unexpected development was that some of the robots began to trick their companions, lighting up when they found poison instead of food. Other robots would speed over, sample the poison, and die, while the liars would move on to a food source and survive. The findings disproved a long-held belief that machines cannot learn to deceive. The idea of a selfish robot that tells fibs is troubling, but not all the robots in the Swiss experiment turned bad. Heroic robots also emerged, ones that signaled danger to their peers and put themselves in harm's way to save another. The experiment inspired both wariness and hope for the future of robotics.

sensitive areas open up, and it is the specific responsibility of the scientists who work in this field to face this new array of social and ethical problems."[73]

Robots of the Future

The need to protect future societies from unethical robots may put constraints on technology that is intended to help people. Not all roboticists agree with the dire predictions that robots could endanger humanity, however. Most see the numerous benefits robots could have in society. "We have a really good chance of constructing a comfortable retirement for ourselves,"[74] says Moravec, describing a society in which robots could one day perform nearly all tasks that are dangerous or distasteful to people and could even work side by side with humans to create a better and more comfortable world. Most scientists agree that the rise of autonomous robots with human-level intelligence is not only possible in the next generation, but inevitable. Already, says futurist and inventor Ray Kurzweil, the human brain is something scientists can finally fathom and manage. "We can reasonably forecast that there will be exhaustive models and simulations of all several hundred regions of the human brain within about 20 years," he says, predicting that "we will have both the hardware and software to achieve human-level intelligence in a machine by 2029."[75]

What human inventors do with a newly created, intelligent life form holds a great deal of promise. Already, robots like Asimo, a humanlike robotic servant made by the Japanese company Honda, are working in office environments to show human visitors around buildings, serve refreshments during meetings, and perform other tasks a human office assistant might do. The International Federation of Robotics predicts that in 2011, more than 12 million robots will be performing various services in people's homes and businesses around the world. By the year 2020, robots may account for 30 percent of the U.S. Army, according to a report by researchers at Washington University in St. Louis, Missouri. "It is reasonable to assume that by 2050," says Kaku, "we may have robots that can interface intelligibly with humans . . . we will be able to talk with them and have relatively interesting conversations."[76]

In the hands of their creators, robots are catching up to the intelligence possessed by humans. "Once they do catch up," says Moravec, "then they keep on going. . . . Ultimately, I think they're on their own and they'll do things that we can't imagine or understand . . . just the way children do."[77] Already, at Robert Gordon University in the United Kingdom, scientists have created a computerized robotic brain that adds new learning modules and becomes more complex every time the robot is programmed to do something new. This robot, although very simple, is growing more intelligent over time—in other words, with the help of roboticists, its brain is evolving. If robots eventually reach the point at which their brains and behavior can evolve without any interference from people, human beings will have created a new, artificial species, perhaps one that is even smart enough to reproduce. "Once robots are in the wild, they can evolve on their own," says computer scientist Bill Joy, cofounder of

Sun Microsystems. "They're likely to outevolve us. . . . I don't think that's something we should do lightly."[78] Not everyone agrees that robots could one day become the dominant species on Earth, but one thing is clear: Robotics is a rapidly advancing field of technology that is changing the world and the human experience. It poses great promise as well as great responsibility for people of the future.

NOTES

Chapter 1:
The History of Robots

1. Lisa Nocks, *The Robot: The Life Story of a Technology,* Westport, CT: Greenwood, 2007, p. 5.
2. Nocks, *Robot,* p. 7.
3. Nocks, *Robot,* p. 13.
4. Mark E. Rosheim, *Robot Evolution: The Development of Anthrobiotics,* Hoboken, NJ: Wiley, 1994, p. 18.
5. Rosheim, *Robot Evolution,* p. 29.
6. Rosheim, *Robot Evolution,* p. 3.
7. Rosheim, *Robot Evolution,* p. 37.
8. Michael White, *Isaac Asimov: A Life of the Grand Master of Science Fiction,* New York: Carroll and Graf, 1994, pp. 55–56.
9. John Johnston, *The Allure of Machinic Life: Cybernetics, Artificial Life, and the New AI,* Cambridge, MA: MIT Press, 2008, pp. 49–50.
10. Maja J. Matarić, *The Robotics Primer,* Cambridge, MA: MIT Press, 2007, p. 11.
11. Matarić, *Robotics Primer,* p. 14.
12. Rodney A. Brooks, *Cambrian Intelligence: The Early History of the New AI,* Cambridge, MA: MIT Press, 1999, p. 151.
13. Brooks, *Cambrian Intelligence,* p. vii.
14. Brooks, *Cambrian Intelligence,* p. ix.
15. Matarić, *Robotics Primer,* p. 15.
16. Alden P. Armagnac, "New Factory Worker: Teachable Robot Can Remember 200 Commands," *Popular Science,* August 1962, p. 81.
17. Armagnac, "New Factory Worker," p. 81.

Chapter 2:
How Robots Move

18. Mark E. Rosheim, *Leonardo's Lost Robots,* New York: Springer, 2006, p. 19.
19. Paul E. Sandin, *Robot Mechanisms and Mechanical Devices Illustrated,* New York: McGraw-Hill, 2003, p. xi.
20. Charles M. Bergren, *Anatomy of a Robot,* New York: McGraw-Hill, 2003, p. xii.
21. Rosheim, *Robot Evolution,* p. xii.
22. Rosheim, *Robot Evolution,* p. 40.
23. Brooks, *Cambrian Intelligence,* p. 10.
24. Sandin, *Robot Mechanisms,* p. xi.

25. Sandin, *Robot Mechanisms*, p. xi.

26. Sandin, *Robot Mechanisms*, p. 230.

27. Matarić, *Robotics Primer*, p. 39.

28. Sandin, *Robot Mechanisms*, p. 201.

29. Brooks, *Cambrian Intelligence*, p. 27.

30. Gordon McComb and Myke Predko, *Robot Builder's Bonanza*, 3rd ed., Columbus, OH: McGraw-Hill, 2006, p. 16.

31. McComb and Predko, *Robot Builder's Bonanza*, p. 277.

32. Sandin, *Robot Mechanism*, p. xiii.

33. Gareth Branwyn, *Absolute Beginner's Guide to Building Robots*, Toronto, Ontario: Que, 2004, p. 96.

34. Quoted in Anna Austin, "Biomass-Based Robot to Feed, Power Itself," *Biomass Magazine*, April 2009, www.biomassmagazine.com/article.jsp?article_id=2530.

Chapter 3: How Robots Think

35. Matarić, *Robotics Primer*, p. 25.

36. McComb and Predko, *Robot Builder's Bonanza*, p. 151.

37. McComb and Predko, *Robot Builder's Bonanza*, p. 155.

38. Marcus Hutter, *Universal Artificial Intelligence: Sequential Decisions Based on Algorithmic Probability*, New York: Springer, 2005, p. 2.

39. McComb and Predko, *Robot Builder's Bonanza*, p. 169.

40. Brooks, *Cambrian Intelligence*, p. 35.

41. Hans P. Moravec, *Robot: Mere Machine to Transcendent Mind*, New York: Oxford University Press, 1999, p. 17.

42. Moravec, *Robot*, p. 87.

43. Quoted in Larry Laufenberg, "Robonaut Provides Hands-On Assistance in Space," *Infusion*, Mountain View, CA: NASA Computing, Information, and Communications Technology Program, pp. 1–2.

44. Josh Joseph and Brandon Luders, "Modelling and Simulation of Robot Proprioception from Sensor Data," graduate paper, Massachusetts Institute of Technology, December 8, 2006, http://web.mit.edu/luders/www/work/proprio_paper.pdf.

45. Henrik I. Christensen and Gregory D. Hager, "Sensing and Estimation," in *Springer Handbook of Robotics*, eds. Bruno Siciliano and Oussama Khatib, Berlin, Germany: Springer, 2008, pp. 87–108, 87.

46. Mark Moll and Daniela Rus, "Editorial: Special Issue on Self-Reconfiguring Modular Robots," *International Journal of Robotics Research* 27, no. 3–4, March–April 2008, pp. 277–78.

Chapter 4: How Robots Are Used

47. Lev Grossman, "Maid to Order," *Time*, September 14, 2002, www.time.com/time/roomba.

48. Justin Mullins, "Sewer Robot Learns to Do Our Dirty Work," *NewScientist*, June 17, 2000, www.newscientist.com/article/

learns-to-do-our-dirty-work.html.

49. David Crowder, Gerald Bauer, and Donald Young, "Inspecting Large Sewers," *Trenchless International*, May 29, 2009, http://trenchlessinternational.com/news/inspecting_large_sewers/00858.

50. M.F. Silva and J.A.T. Machado, "Climbing Robots: A Survey of Technologies and Applications," in *Advances in Mobile Robotics: Proceedings of the Eleventh International Conference on Climbing and Walking Robots and the Support Technology for Mobile Machines*, eds. L. Marques, A. de Almeida, M.O. Tokhi, and G.S. Virk, Hackensack, NJ: World Scientific, 2008, pp. 1133–40, 1134.

51. Quoted in Asian News International, "Novel Robots to Traverse Potentially Dangerous Ice Environments," Thaindian News, May 28, 2008, www.thaindian.com/newsportal/india-news/novel-robots-to-traverse-potentially-dangerous-ice-environments_10053786.html.

52. Carnegie Mellon Robotics Institute, "Dante II: Overview," Carnegie Mellon Robotics Institute, www.ri.cmu.edu/research_project_detail.html?project_id=163&menu_id=261.

53. David Shukman, "ISIS Robot Sub Explores Giant Canyon off Portugal," CDNN, June 19, 2007, www.cdnn.info/news/science/sc070619.html.

54. Shukman, "ISIS Robot Sub Explores Giant Canyon off Portugal."

55. Quoted in BBC News, "Robot Sub Reaches Deepest Ocean," BBC News, June 3, 2009, http://news.bbc.co.uk/2/hi/science/nature/8080324.stm.

56. Kuchera Engineering, "teleMax: The World's Most Advanced EOD Robot," brochure, Kuchera Engineering, www.kuchera.com/ke/products/robotics/telemax.pdf.

57. Quoted in Johns Hopkins University, "Students Design Land Mine Robot: Low-Cost Rover May Aid in Land Mine Detection," news release, June 8, 2004, www.jhu.edu/news_info/news/audio-video/mediamines.html.

58. Quoted in SRI International, "DARPA Selects SRI International to Lead Trauma Pod Battlefield Medical Treatment System Development Program," news release, March 28, 2005, www.sri.com/news/releases/03-28-05.html.

Chapter 5: A Society Shared by Robots

59. Michio Kaku, *Visions: How Science Will Revolutionize the 21st Century and Beyond*, Oxford, England: Oxford University Press, 1998, p. 91.

60. Quoted in NOVA Online, *Bomb Squad: Hans Moravec*, NOVA Online, October 1997, www.pbs.org/wgbh/nova/robots/moravec.html.

61. Cynthia Breazeal and Rodney Brooks, "Robot Emotion: A Functional

Perspective," in *Who Needs Emotions? The Brain Meets the Robot*, eds. Jean-Marc Fellous and Michael A. Arbib, New York: Oxford University Press, 2005, pp. 274–306, 279.

62. Quoted in ScienceDaily, "Designing a Robot That Can Sense Human Emotion," ScienceDaily, December 16, 2002, www.sciencedaily.com/releases/2002/12/021216070618.htm.

63. Breazeal and Brooks, "Robot Emotion," p. 282.

64. Personal Robots Group, "Social Learning in Physical and Virtual Worlds," Personal Robots Group, http://robotic.media.mit.edu/projects/robots/mds/social/social.html.

65. Personal Robots Group, "Social Learning in Physical and Virtual Worlds."

66. George A. Bekey, *Autonomous Robots: From Biological Inspiration to Implementation and Control*, Cambridge, MA: MIT Press, 2005, p. 441.

67. Bekey, *Autonomous Robots*, pp. 511–12.

68. Bergren, *Anatomy of a Robot*, p. 136.

69. A.O. Scott, "In a World Left Silent, One Heart Beeps," *New York Times*, June 27, 2008, http://movies.nytimes.com/2008/06/27/movies/27wall.html.

70. Bergren, *Anatomy of a Robot*, p. 135.

71. Bekey, *Autonomous Robots*, p. 516.

72. Bekey, *Autonomous Robots*, p. 513.

73. Quoted in Stefan Lovgren, "Robot Code of Ethics to Prevent Android Abuse, Protect Humans," *National Geographic*, March 16, 2007, http://news.nationalgeographic.com/news/2007/03/070316-robot-ethics.html.

74. Quoted in "Future 'Bots: Robot-Human Convergence Begins," video, written by Rob Goldberg, produced by Thomas Lucas, LiveScience, www.livescience.com/common/media/video/player.php?aid=26545.

75. Ray Kurzweil, "The Future of Robots," PopSci, September 1, 2006, www.popsci.com/scitech/article/2006-09/future-robots?page=1.

76. Kaku, *Visions*, p. 90.

77. Quoted in NOVA Online, *Bomb Squad*.

78. Quoted in Goldberg, "Future 'Bots."

GLOSSARY

actuation: The setting in motion of robotic parts.

actuator: A mechanical device that acts as a robot's muscles to move parts like arms and wheels.

anatomy: The study of the shape and structure of living organisms.

artificial intelligence: The imitation of intelligent behaviors and human-like thinking in computers and machines.

autonomous: Existing or acting independently.

axle: A shaft with wheels on both ends that turn when the shaft turns.

battery: A device that uses chemicals to create an electrical charge and provide power for a machine.

chassis: A robot's body.

cogwheel: A wheel with pegs, notches, or teeth along its outer edge.

computer: An electronic device that processes and stores data and can be programmed to do certain tasks.

degree of freedom: A single direction in which a joint can bend or rotate, such as up and down or side to side.

ethics: Moral principles and values; a sense of right or wrong.

fuel cell: A type of battery that takes hydrogen and oxygen from the environment and uses them as fuel to create an electrical charge.

gear: A device in which toothed wheels (cogwheels) work against each other to create movement.

hydraulic: Operated by liquid pressure, usually when liquid is forced through a tube.

inclined plane: A sloped surface leading from one level to another; a ramp.

Industrial Revolution: The rapid development of industry that occurred in Britain in the 1800s and 1900s that was brought about by the introduction of machines, factories, and mass production.

infrared sensor: A device that senses differences in heat energy, imperceptible to the human eye.

input: Information put into a data-processing machine (a computer).

joint: A place where two parts are joined together.

linear actuator: An actuator that moves robot parts in a straight line.

machine: A device that transmits force, motion, or energy to perform a task.

motor: A power unit that generates energy to make a machine's parts move.

output: The information or action delivered by a data-processing machine (a computer) after it receives input.

perception: Awareness of things in the environment, gained through physical senses like sight and touch.

peripheral vision: The ability to see things along the outer edges, or periphery, of the field of vision.

photovoltaic cell: A device that converts light energy into electricity.

physiology: The study of physical processes and functions in all or part of an organism.

pneumatic: Operated by air pressure, usually when air or another gas is forced through a tube.

pneumatic artificial muscle (PAM): A device that inflates with air and deflates to stretch and contract, creating pulling and pushing forces that mimic human muscles.

proprioception: The ability to make sense of one's own physical state; self-awareness.

Renaissance: The revival of arts, literature, and science that took place in Europe from the fourteenth to seventeenth centuries.

robot: A device or machine that can perform tasks without human help.

rotary actuator: An actuator that moves robot parts in a spinning motion.

teleoperation: Control of a robot by a human some distance away, using video, audio, and/or sensory communication.

unmanned ground vehicle (UGV): A robotic vehicle that can drive outdoors over a variety of terrain without human operators onboard.

Books

Roger Bridgman, *Robot*. New York: DK Publishing, 2004. This book examines the history of robots, how they are made, and the many fascinating things robots can do.

Jordan D. Brown, *Robo World: The Story of Robot Designer Cynthia Breazeal*. Washington, DC: Joseph Henry Press, 2006. This biography about one of the world's top robot inventors also describes daily life in a robotics lab and some of the most groundbreaking discoveries in the field of robotics.

Charles Piddock, *Future Tech: From Personal Robots to Motorized Monocycles*. Washington, DC: National Geographic Society, 2009. This book discusses the latest advances in artificial intelligence and robotics.

DVD

FIRST Robotics 2004, DVD, Silver Spring, MD: Discovery Channel, 2007. The Science Channel's original special follows three teams and projects from the 2004 season of the FIRST Robotics international robot-building competition for high school students.

Web Sites

Carnegie Mellon Robotics Academy (www.education.rec.ri.cmu.edu). This Web site features robotics lessons, links to robot events, and free downloadable instructions for building various robots out of LEGOs.

For Inspiration and Recognition of Science and Technology (FIRST) (www.usfirst.org). This Web site describes the mission, history, and goals of FIRST, an international robotics competition for kids in grades K-12, and provides instructions for starting a FIRST team to join the competition.

Museum of Science (www.mos.org/robot). This Web site of the Museum of Science in Boston, Massachusetts, offers a "Design Your Own Robot" exhibit. The interactive robot-building exhibit features detailed instructions for making six robots, as well as preactivity and postactivity questions.

Robotics Research Group (www.robotics.utexas.edu/rrg/learn_more). The Web site of the Robotics Research Group, a program at the University of Texas at Austin, offers information on the history of robots, main concepts in robotics, and three-dimensional simulations of how certain robot parts work.

INDEX

PICTURE CREDITS

Jenny MacKay worked as a science, technical, and medical editor before becoming a full-time freelance writer. She is the author of eight nonfiction books for teens and is currently completing her master of fine arts degree in creative writing. She lives with her husband and two children in northern Nevada, where she was born and raised.